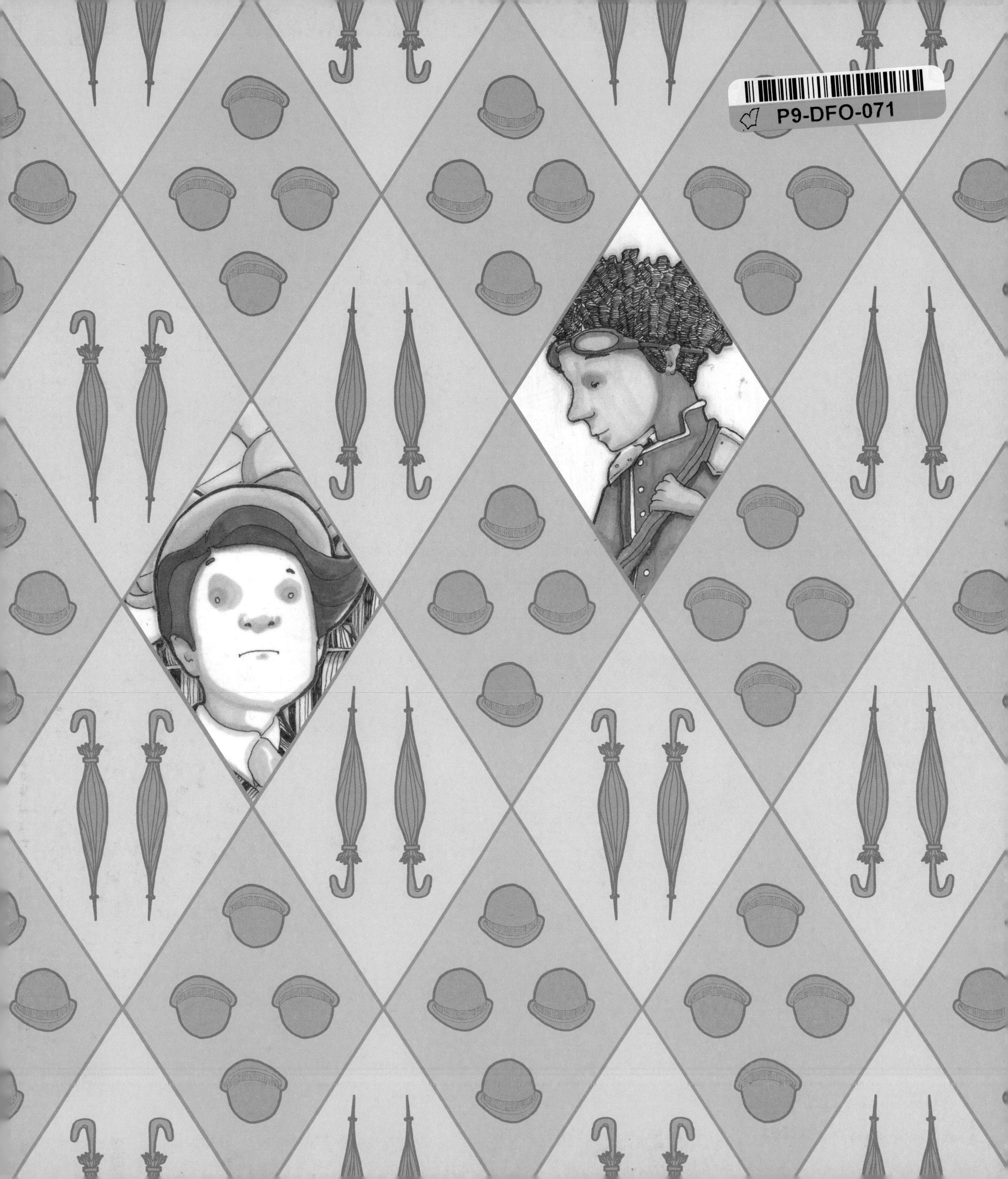

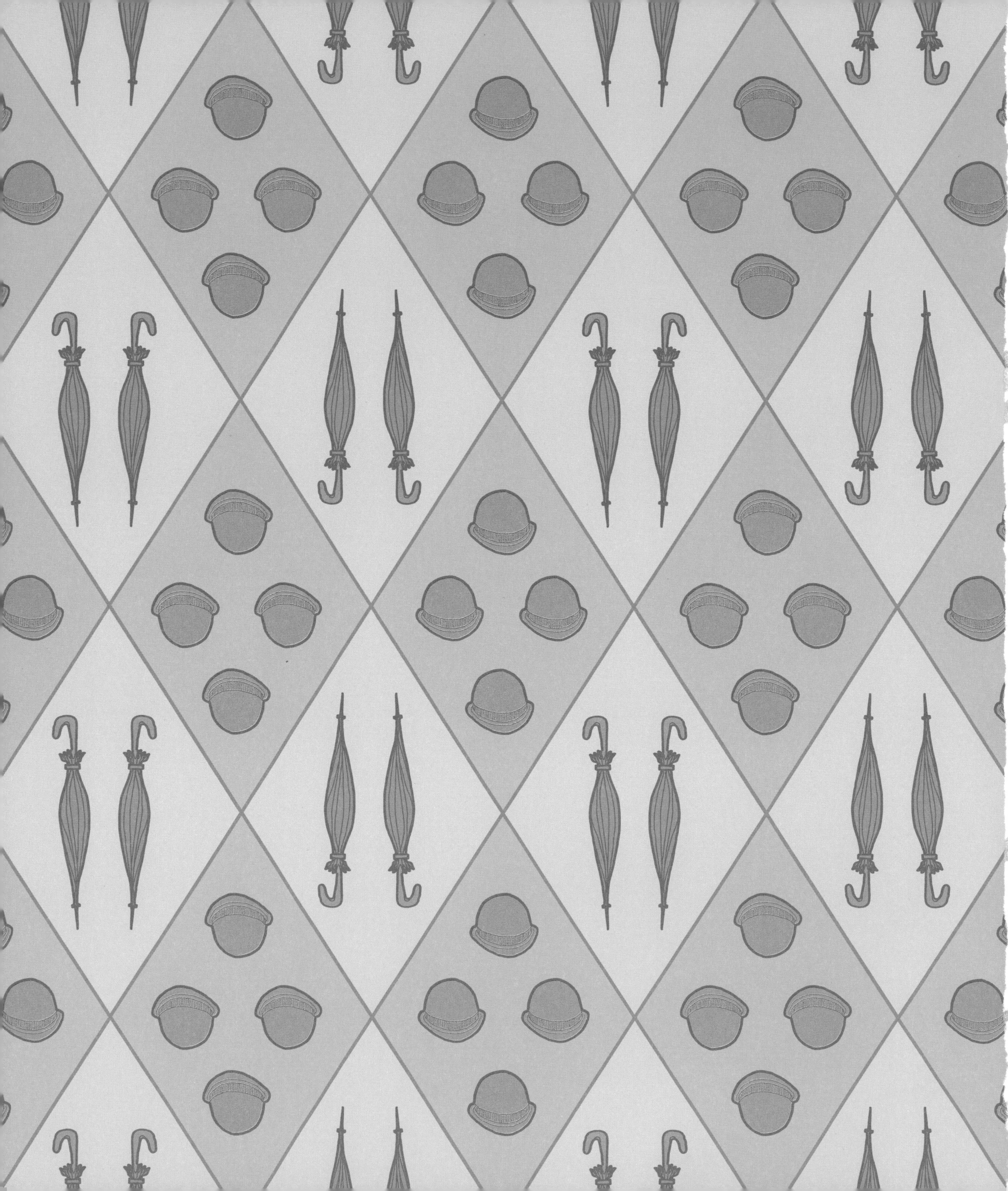

From the Library of

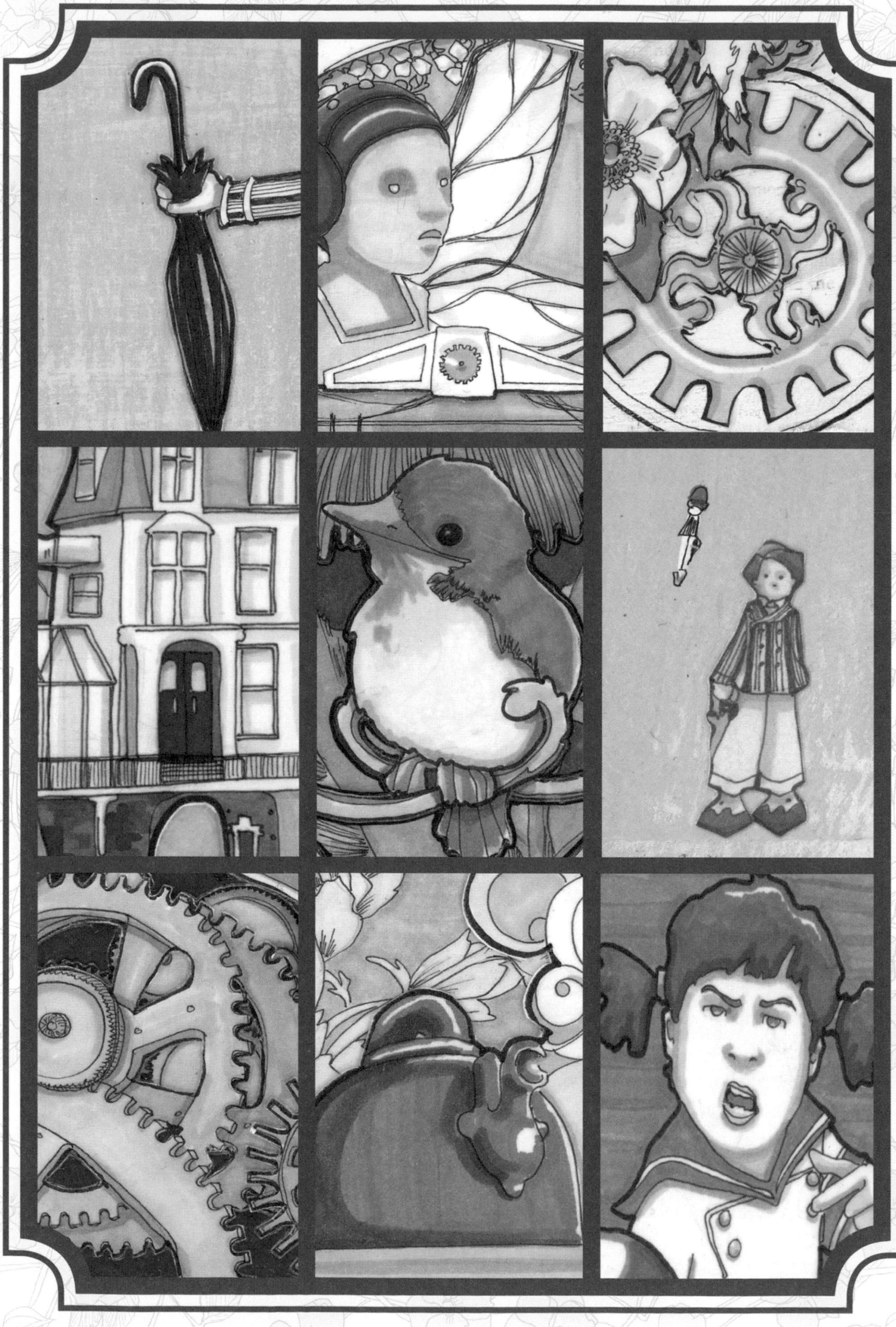

Return of the Dapper Men

written by
Jim McCann

art by
Janet Lee

lettered by
Dave Lanphear

designed by
Todd Klein

production by
Jeremy Brody and Scott Newman

edited by
Stephen Christy

Archaia Comics
Los Angeles

Published by Archaia

Archaia Entertainment, LLC
1680 Vine Street, Suite 912
Los Angeles, CA, 90028
www.archaia.com

ISBN: 1-932386-90-4
ISBN 13: 978-1-932386-90-5

RETURN OF THE DAPPER MEN

November 2010

FIRST PRINTING

10 9 8 7 6 5 4 3 2 1

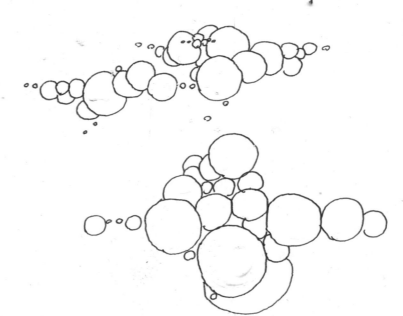

RETURN OF THE DAPPER MEN™
TM and © 2010 Jim McCann and Janet Lee.

Printed in South Korea

For our Michaels.
— Jim and Janet

Special thanks to:
Graphic Artist genius Jeremy Brody, the original dapper man
Tim Gunn, the ever fabulous Gulag Boy, Rebecca Taylor, the
fine folks at Chromatics, composer Jonathan Gjertsen, our
incredibly patient and supportive friends and families, and
the writers & artists whose works continue to inspire our
imaginations everyday.

 INTRODUCTION

By TIM GUNN

I am an avid reader and I love a good story. I'm especially fond of tales that disorient the reader and cause one to question what's real and what isn't. I find stories of this kind to recalibrate my thinking about my place in the world; think *Alice in Wonderland, Through the Looking Glass, The Wizard of Oz*, or even *Pinocchio*.

Accordingly, I am a huge fan of the work of Jim McCann. In my opinion, he is the *ne plus ultra* storyteller — wildly inventive, intelligent, research driven, sharp witted, and he shuns the mundane.

Return of the Dapper Men is a transformational experience, a morality tale that is certain to become an instant contemporary classic. The narrative is instantly captivating and always multi-dimensional. The reader will find puzzles, riddles, and anagrams that serve as catalysts for further investigation and research. Be armed with Google and Merriam-Webster.com in order to enjoy the full-tilt experience of this wondrous read. Furthermore, you'll fall in love with the story's two main characters, Ayden and Zoe, who are part Hansel and Gretel and part Tristan and Isolde.

Then there is the remarkable, breathtaking artwork of Janet Lee. I read Jim's story before seeing Janet's artwork for the book. I found Jim's words to be so vividly visual that it was easy for me to imagine the Big Bang, the topsy-turvy land of Anorev, the visage of Ayden and Zoe, and the Clockwork Angel, which figures prominently and mysteriously in the story. Accordingly, I was apprehensive about seeing Janet's work for fear of disappointment. *Au contraire;* I was rendered speechless by her illustrations — rich and evocative with great depth of surface.

Be prepared to take a fantastic journey. If you're even remotely like me, then you will be permanently altered.

— Tim Gunn

TIM GUNN is an American fashion consultant and television personality, best known as co-host of the Emmy-winning reality show PROJECT RUNWAY. He was the chair of the fashion design department at Parsons The New School for Design and is now the Chief Creative Officer at Liz Claiborne.

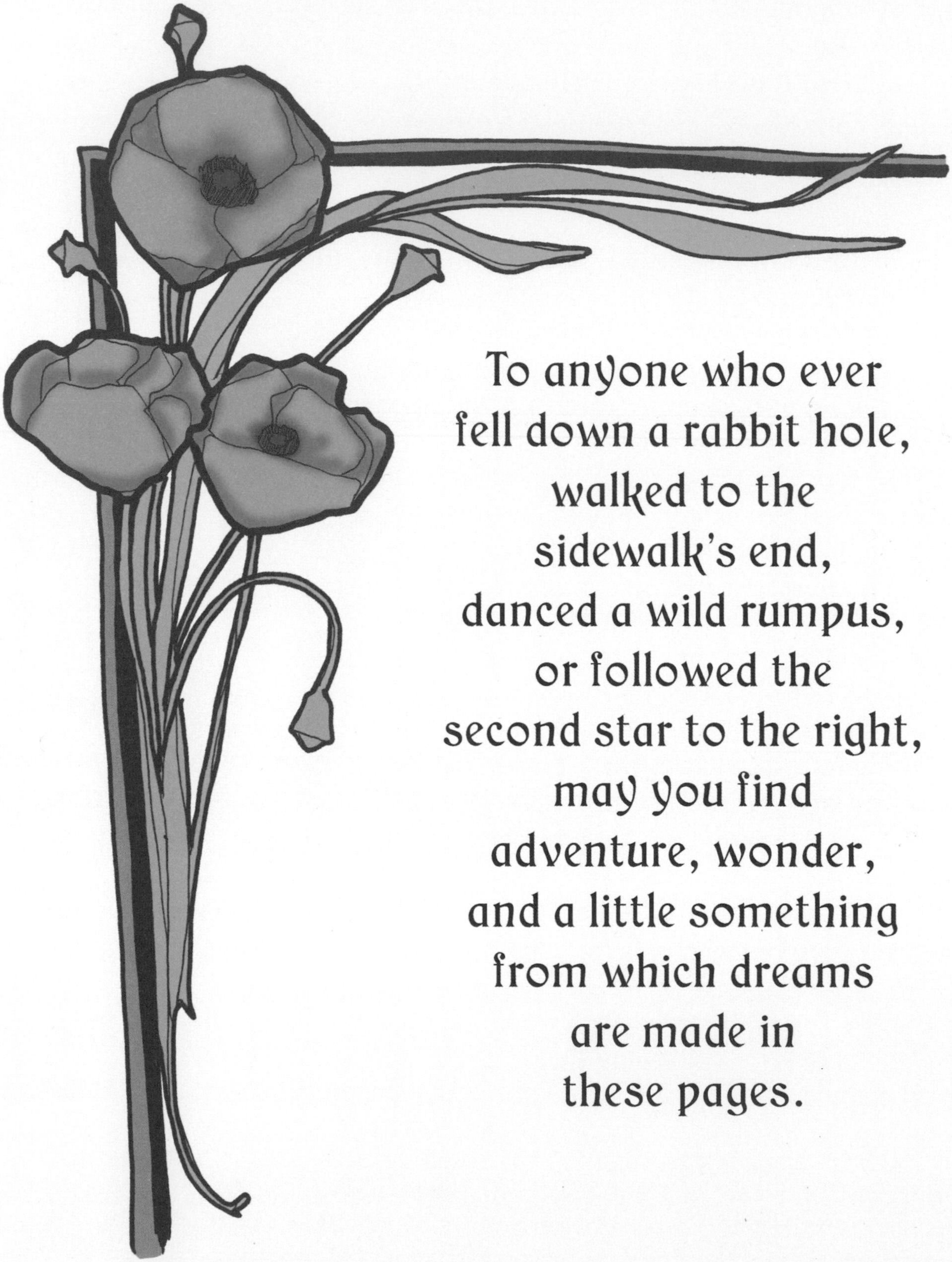

To anyone who ever
fell down a rabbit hole,
walked to the
sidewalk's end,
danced a wild rumpus,
or followed the
second star to the right,
may you find
adventure, wonder,
and a little something
from which dreams
are made in
these pages.

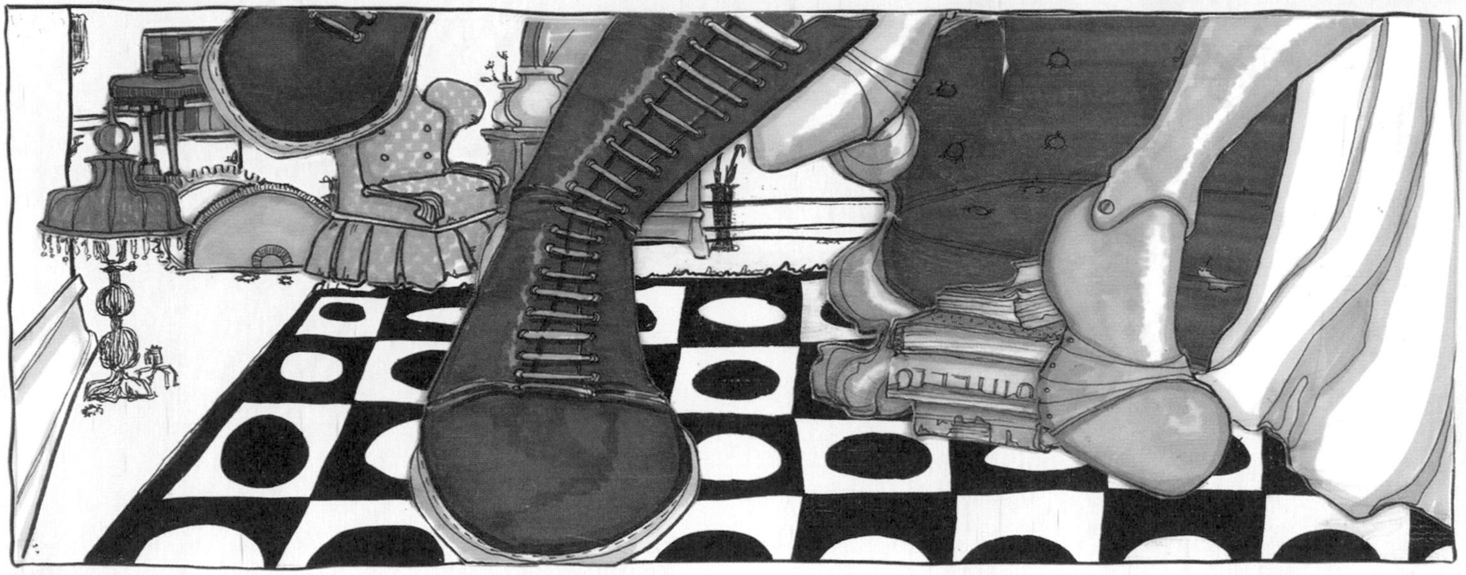

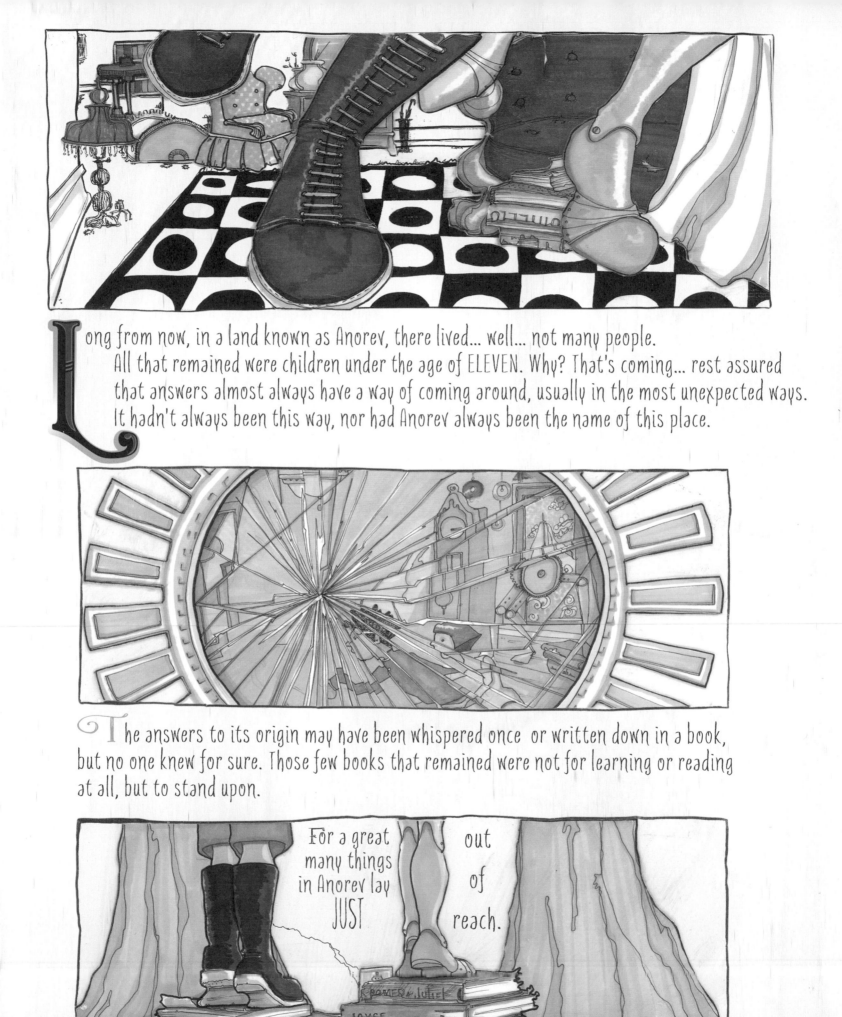

Long from now, in a land known as Anorev, there lived... well... not many people. All that remained were children under the age of ELEVEN. Why? That's coming... rest assured that answers almost always have a way of coming around, usually in the most unexpected ways. It hadn't always been this way, nor had Anorev always been the name of this place.

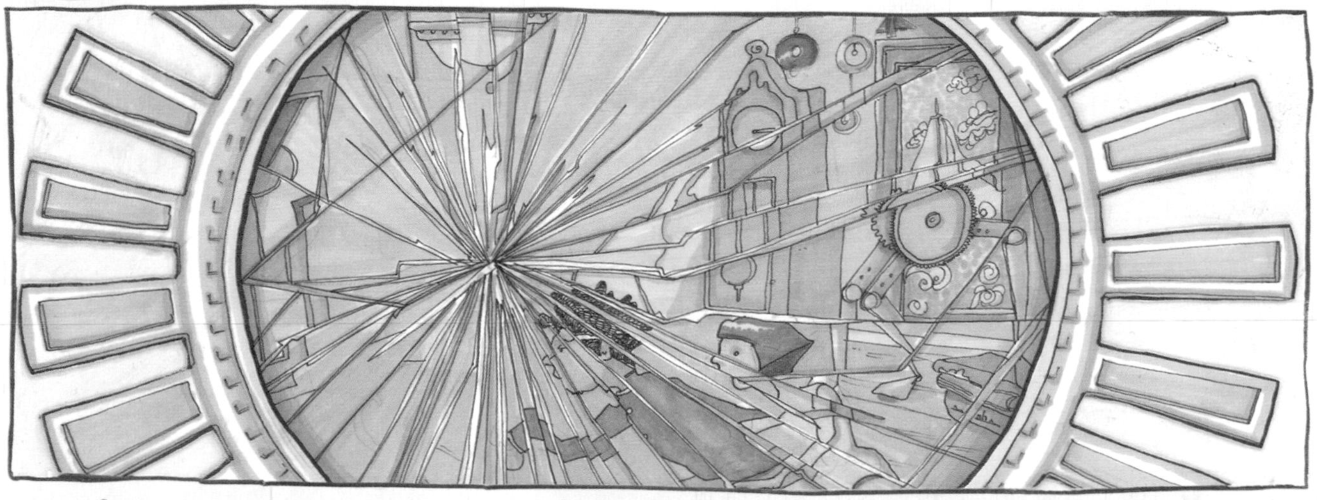

The answers to its origin may have been whispered once or written down in a book, but no one knew for sure. Those few books that remained were not for learning or reading at all, but to stand upon.

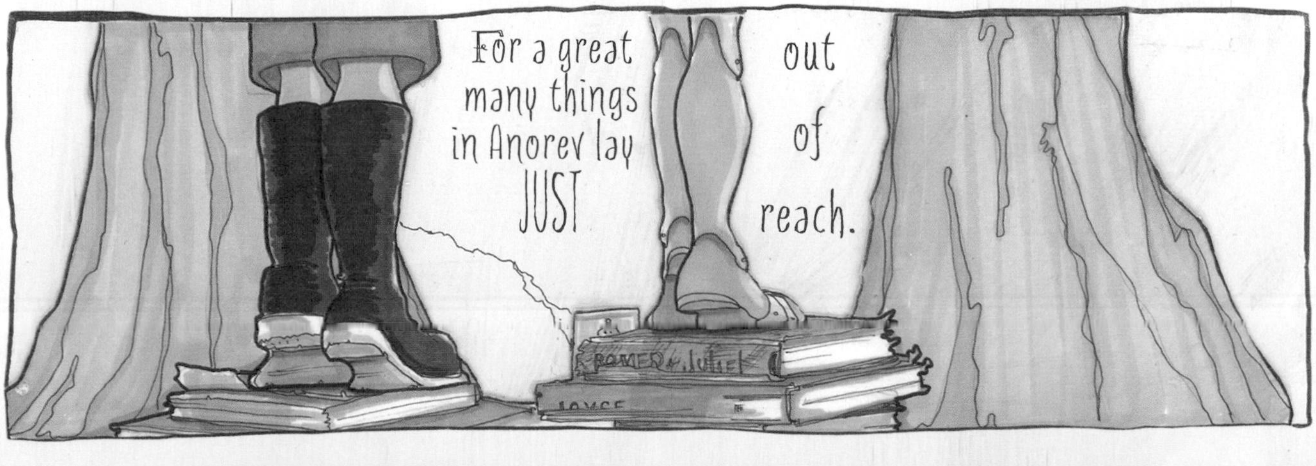
For a great many things in Anorev lay JUST
out of reach.

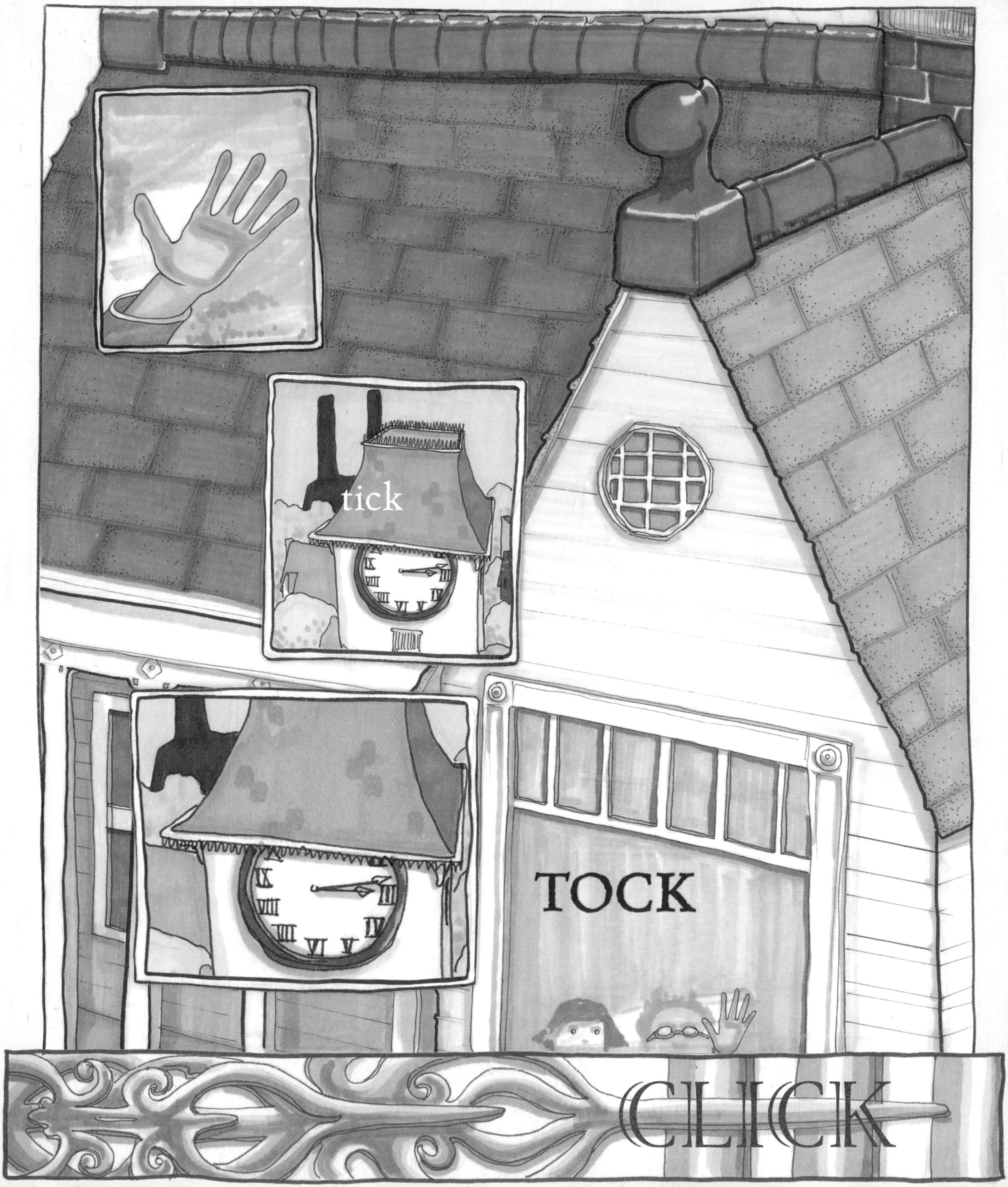
tick
TOCK
CLICK

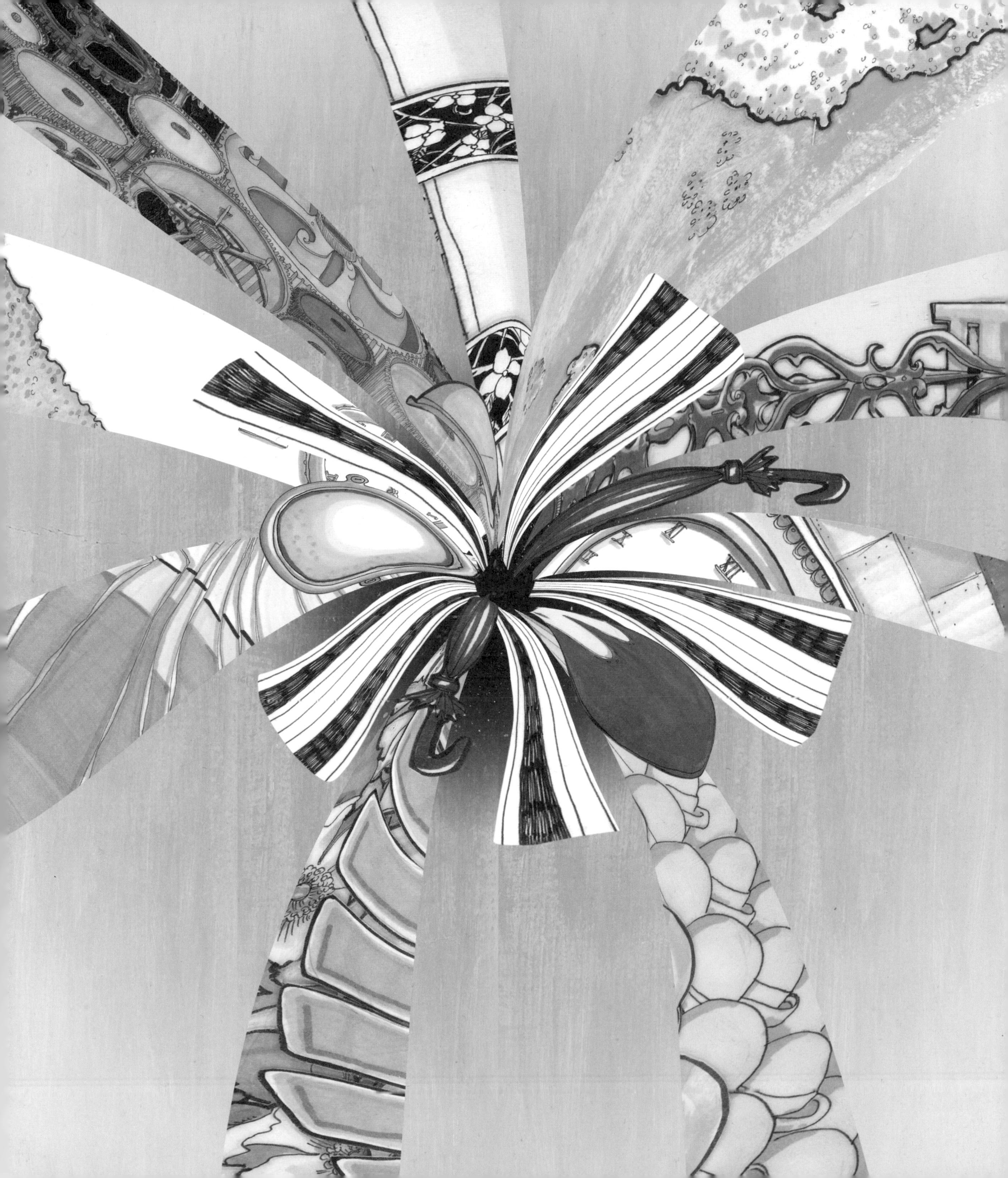

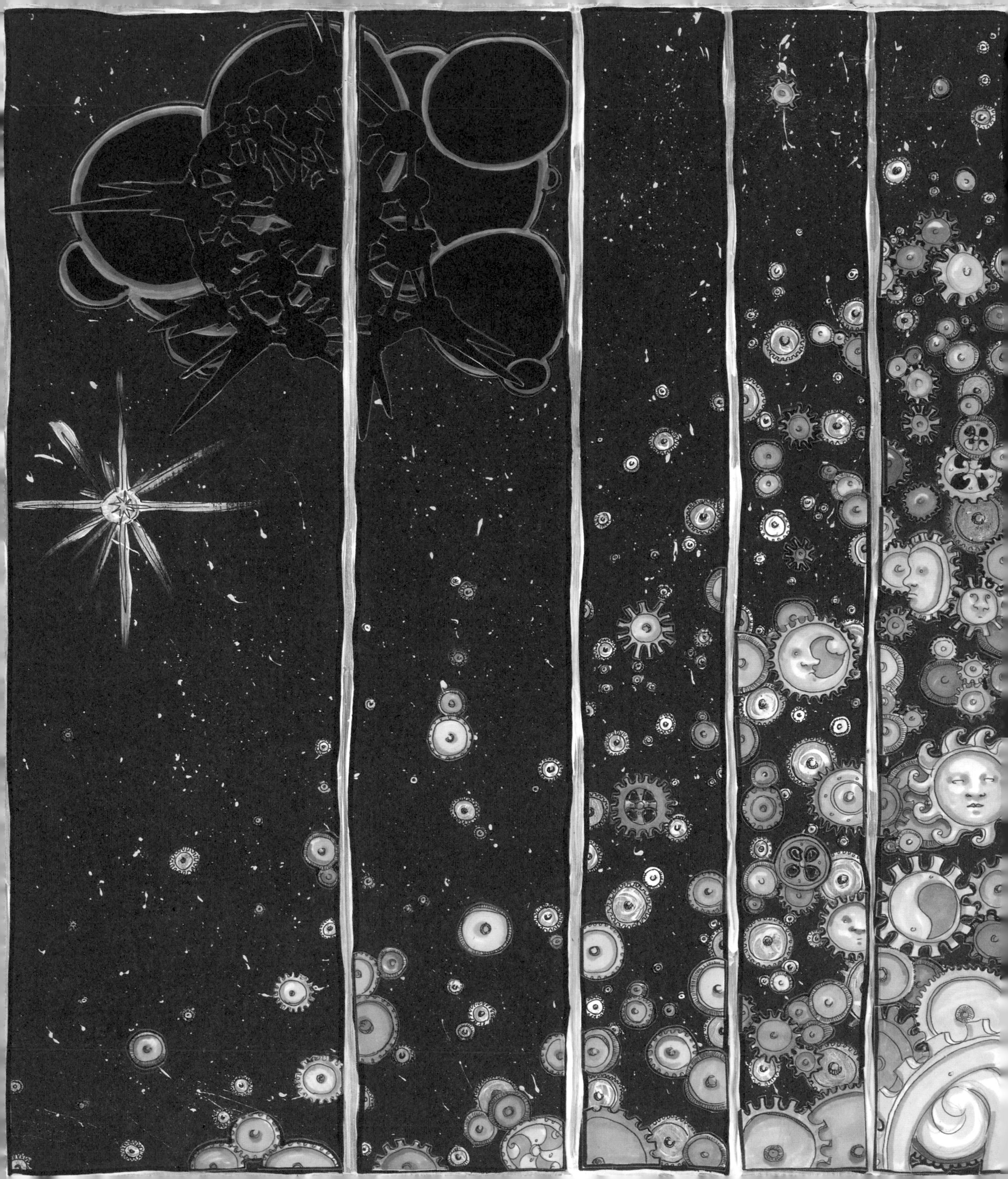

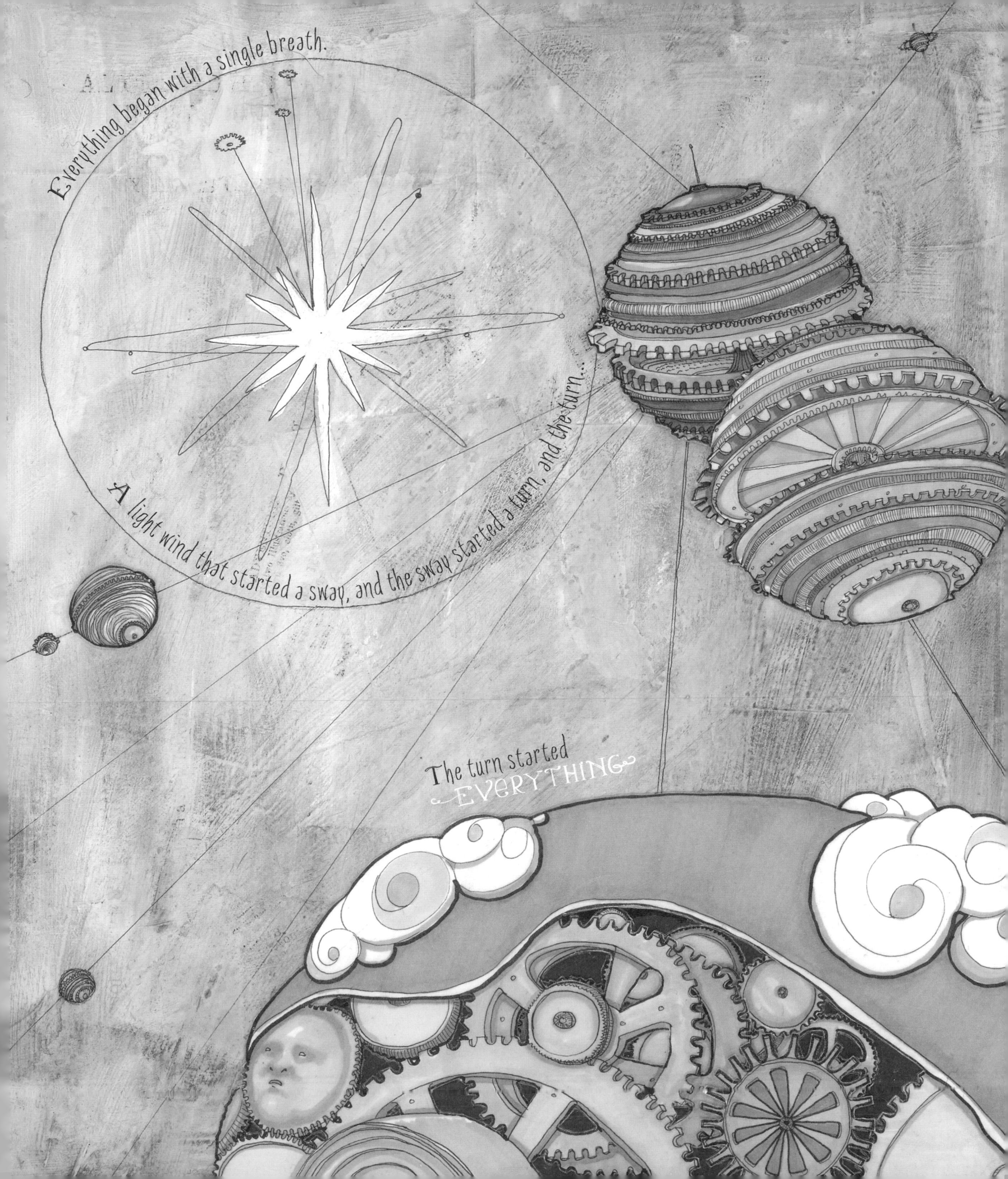

Everything began with a single breath.

A light wind that started a sway, and the sway started a turn, and the turn...

The turn started EVERYTHING

Everything grew and soon needed Time.

Numbers to mark the progress that had been made.

For much had been built and created.

And much had been turned over.

And over.

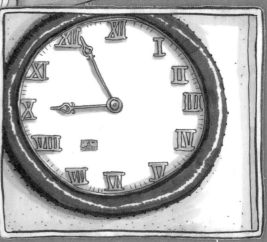

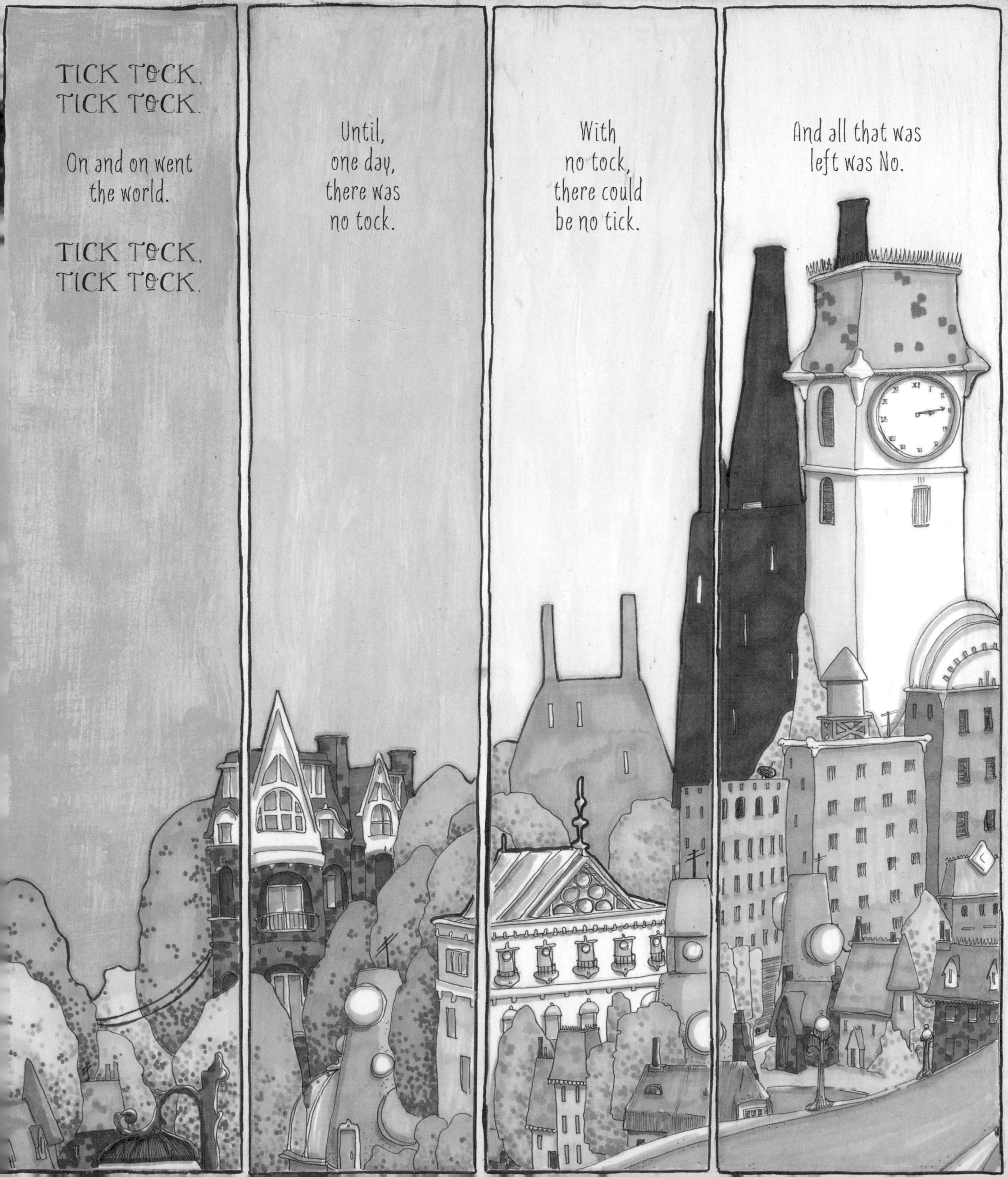
TICK TOCK,
TICK TOCK.
On and on went the world.
TICK TOCK,
TICK TOCK.
Until, one day, there was no tock.
With no tock, there could be no tick.
And all that was left was No.

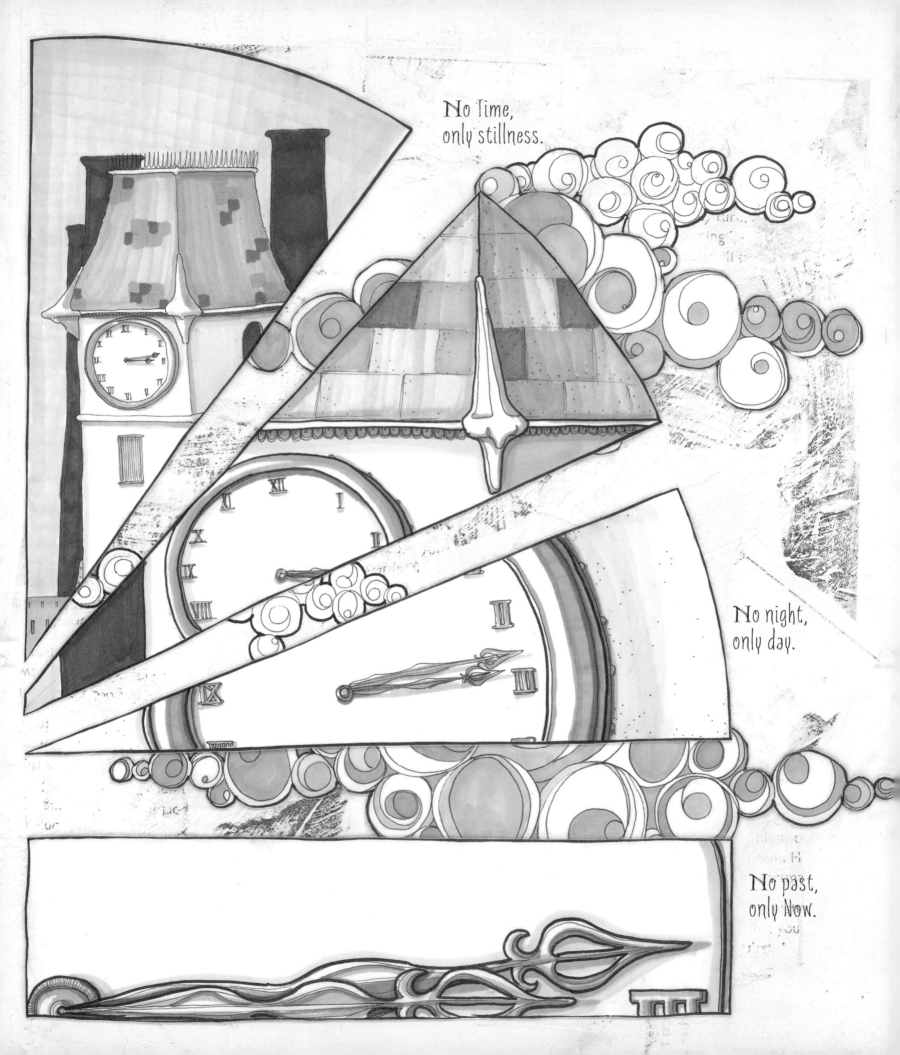

No Time,
only stillness.

No night,
only day.

No past,
only Now.

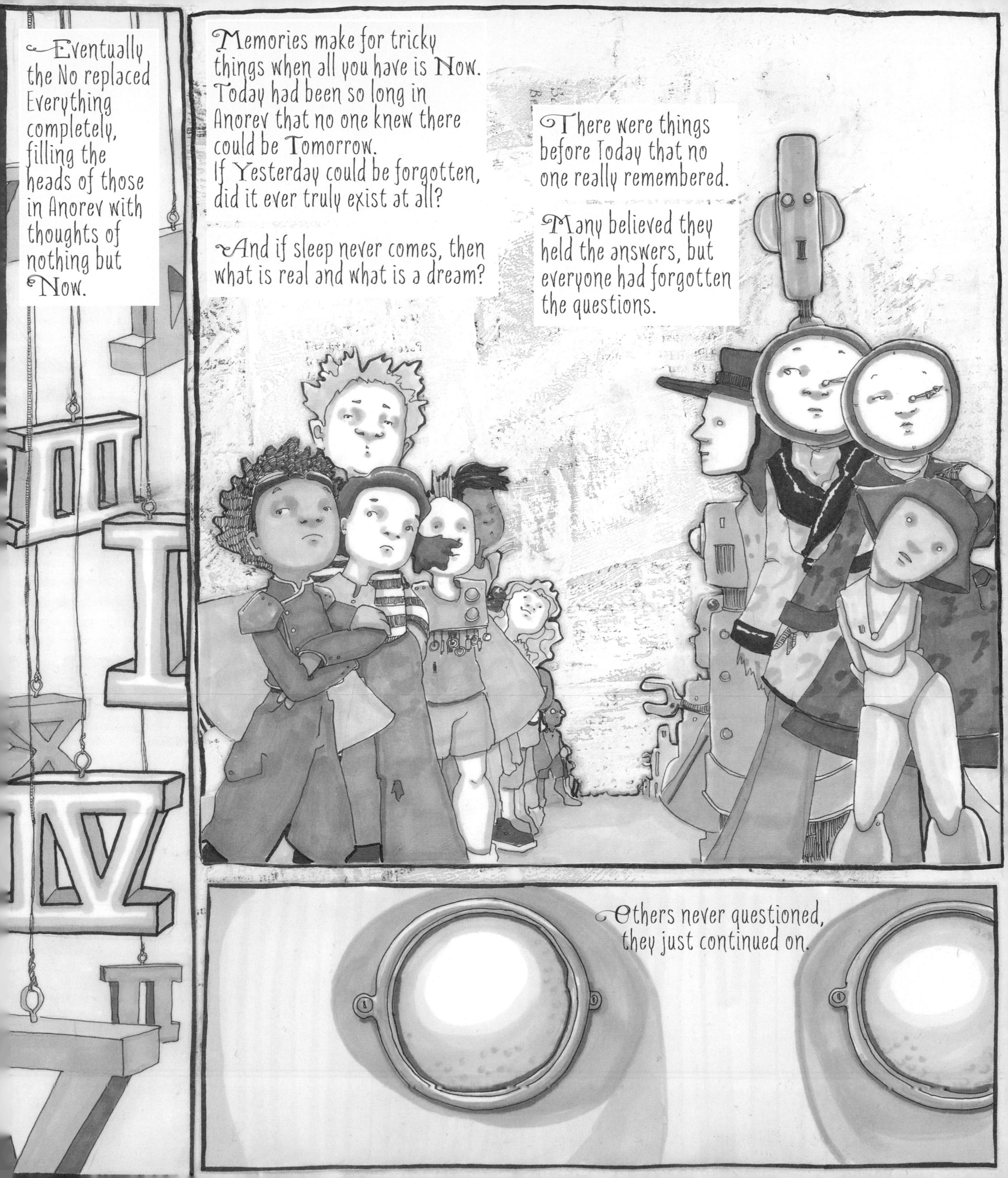
Eventually the No replaced Everything completely, filling the heads of those in Anorev with thoughts of nothing but Now.
Memories make for tricky things when all you have is Now. Today had been so long in Anorev that no one knew there could be Tomorrow. If Yesterday could be forgotten, did it ever truly exist at all?
And if sleep never comes, then what is real and what is a dream?
There were things before Today that no one really remembered.
Many believed they held the answers, but everyone had forgotten the questions.
Others never questioned, they just continued on.

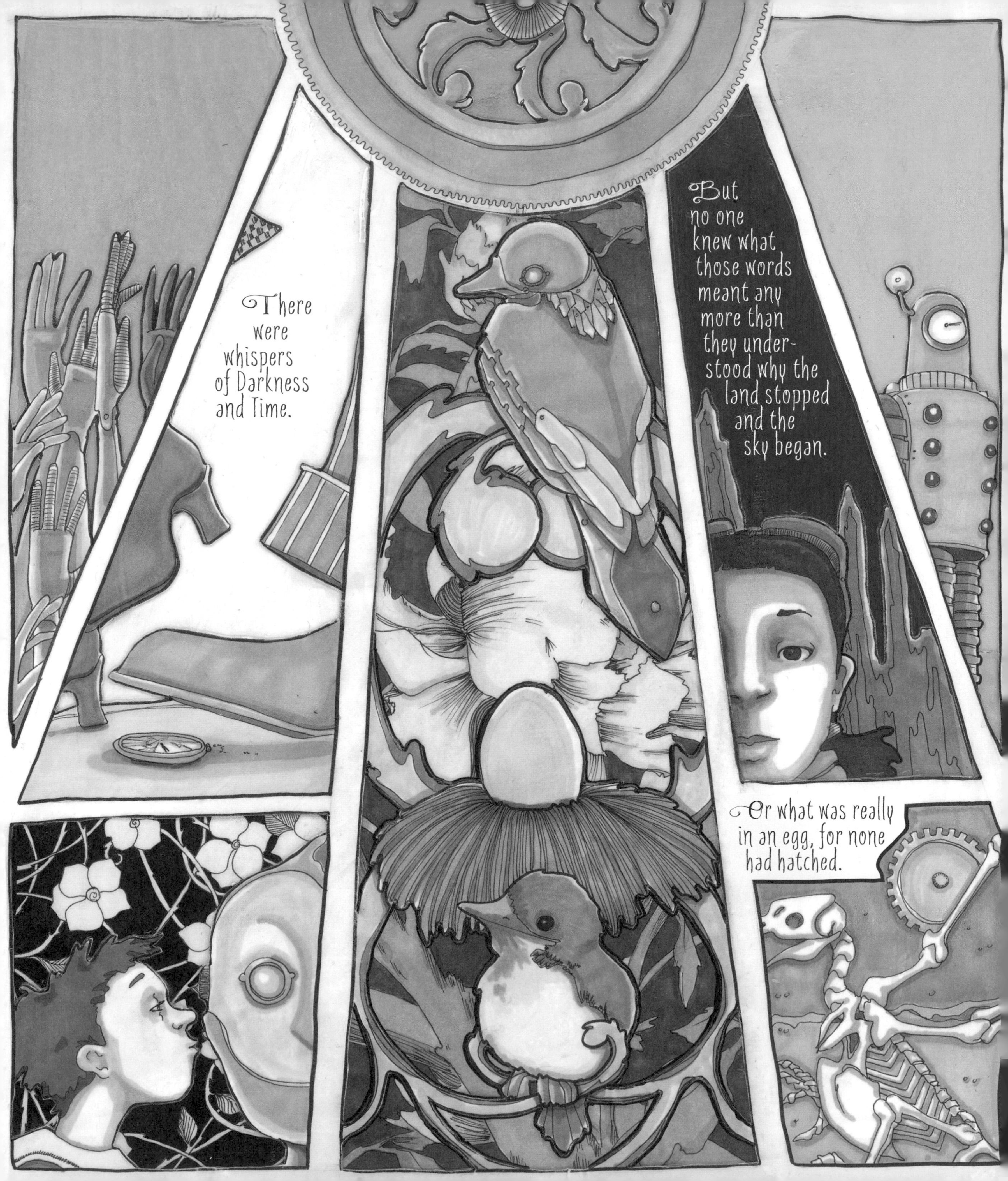
There were whispers of Darkness and Time.
But no one knew what those words meant any more than they under-stood why the land stopped and the sky began.
Or what was really in an egg, for none had hatched.

This was a land of children and machines. Neither knew who made the other and both claimed to be the First.

The children cared for playing and the machines for working--which is how it should be. But with no one to tell them to settle down or stop working, both continued along. And continued. And continued.

And continued.

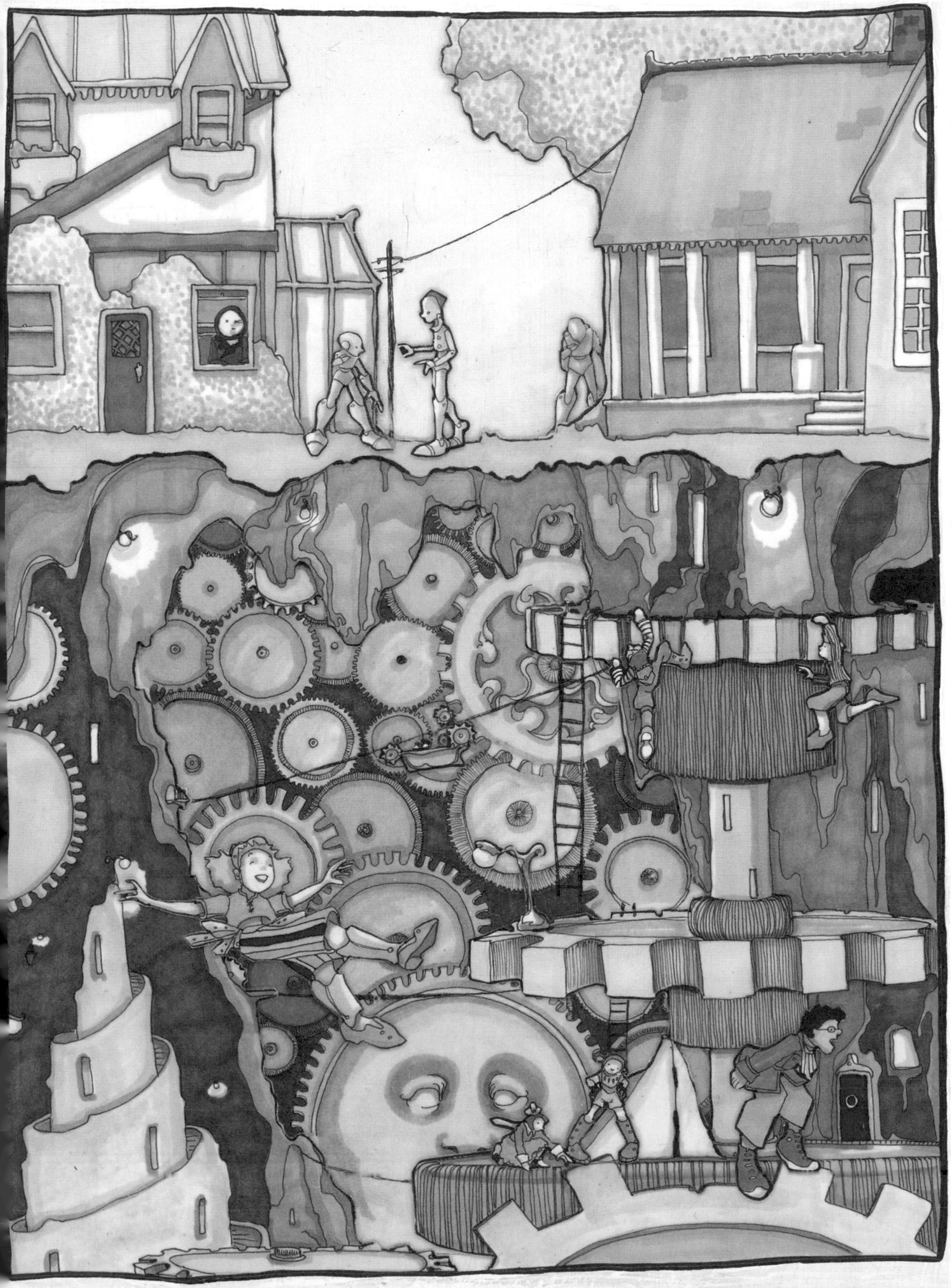

Soon, neither children nor machines knew which was work nor what was play, and neither seemed to be of any fun or any use.

Purpose was lost and both the children and the machines retreated to themselves. The children built a life among the gears of the world and ignored what was above, while the machines lived quietly in homes long abandoned.

They didn't share their knowledge or wisdom nor did they speak of the past, all of which is what makes history.

So that is why what was to come would take them all by surprise.

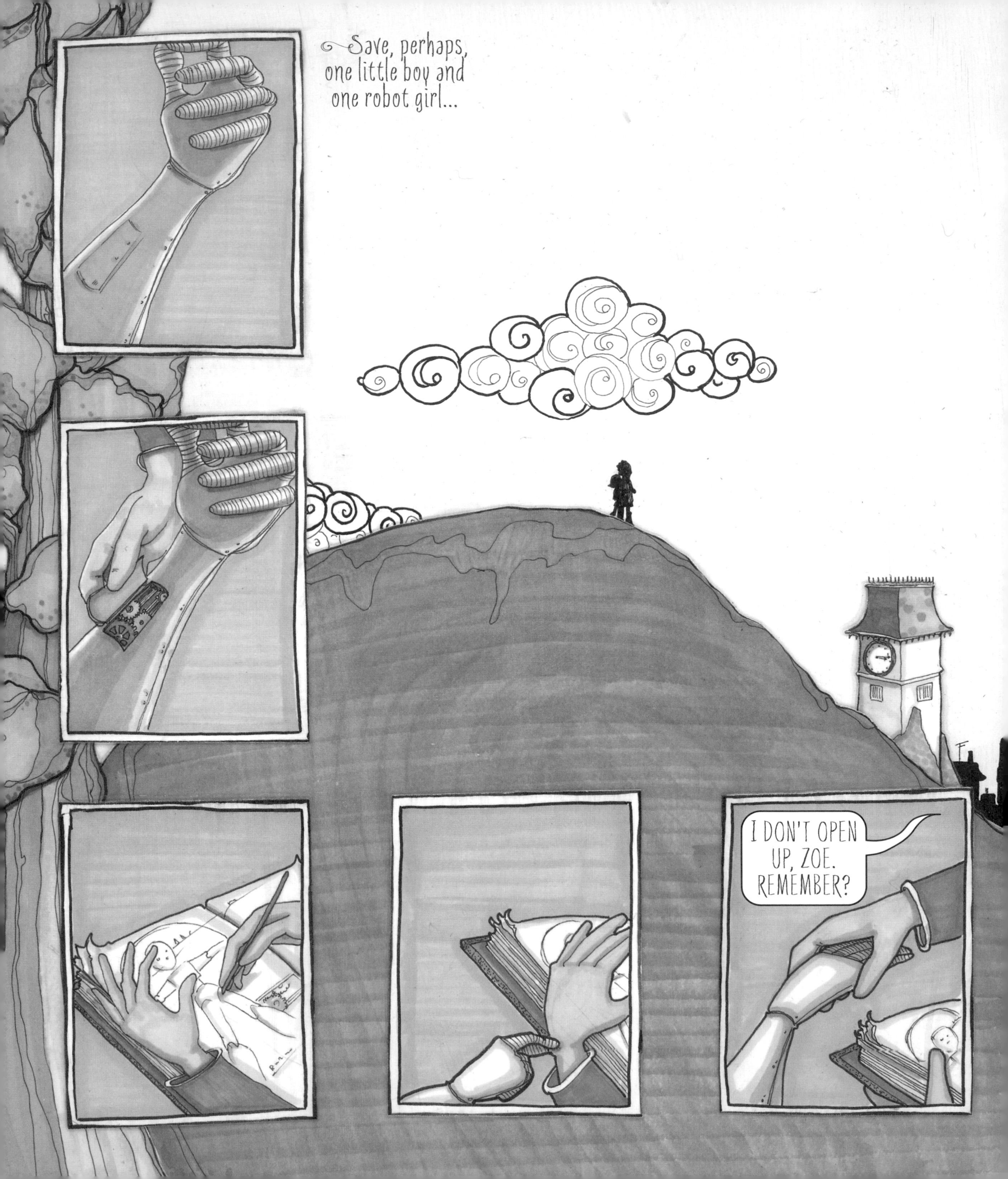
Save, perhaps, one little boy and one robot girl...
I DON'T OPEN UP, ZOE. REMEMBER?

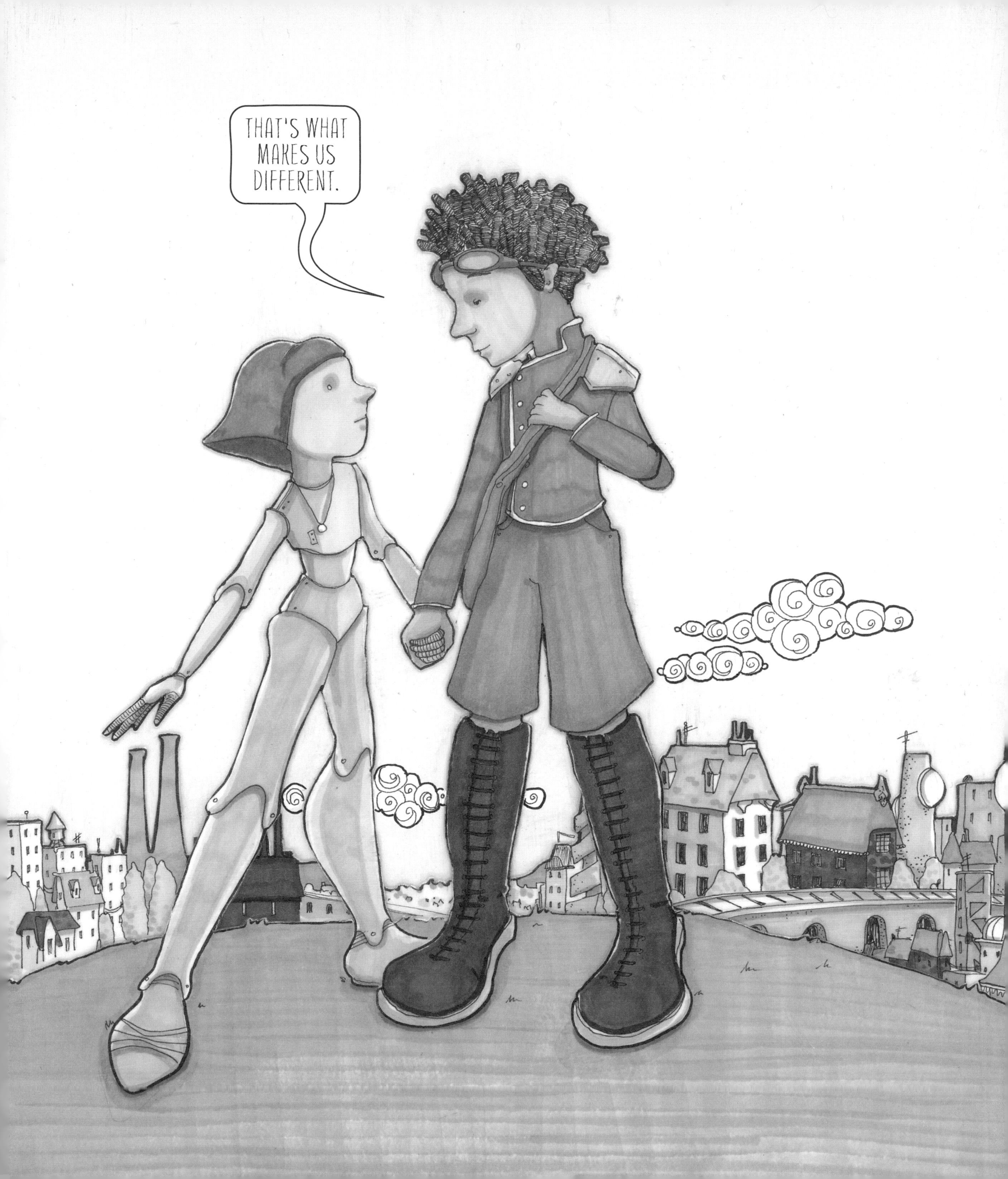
THAT'S WHAT MAKES US DIFFERENT.

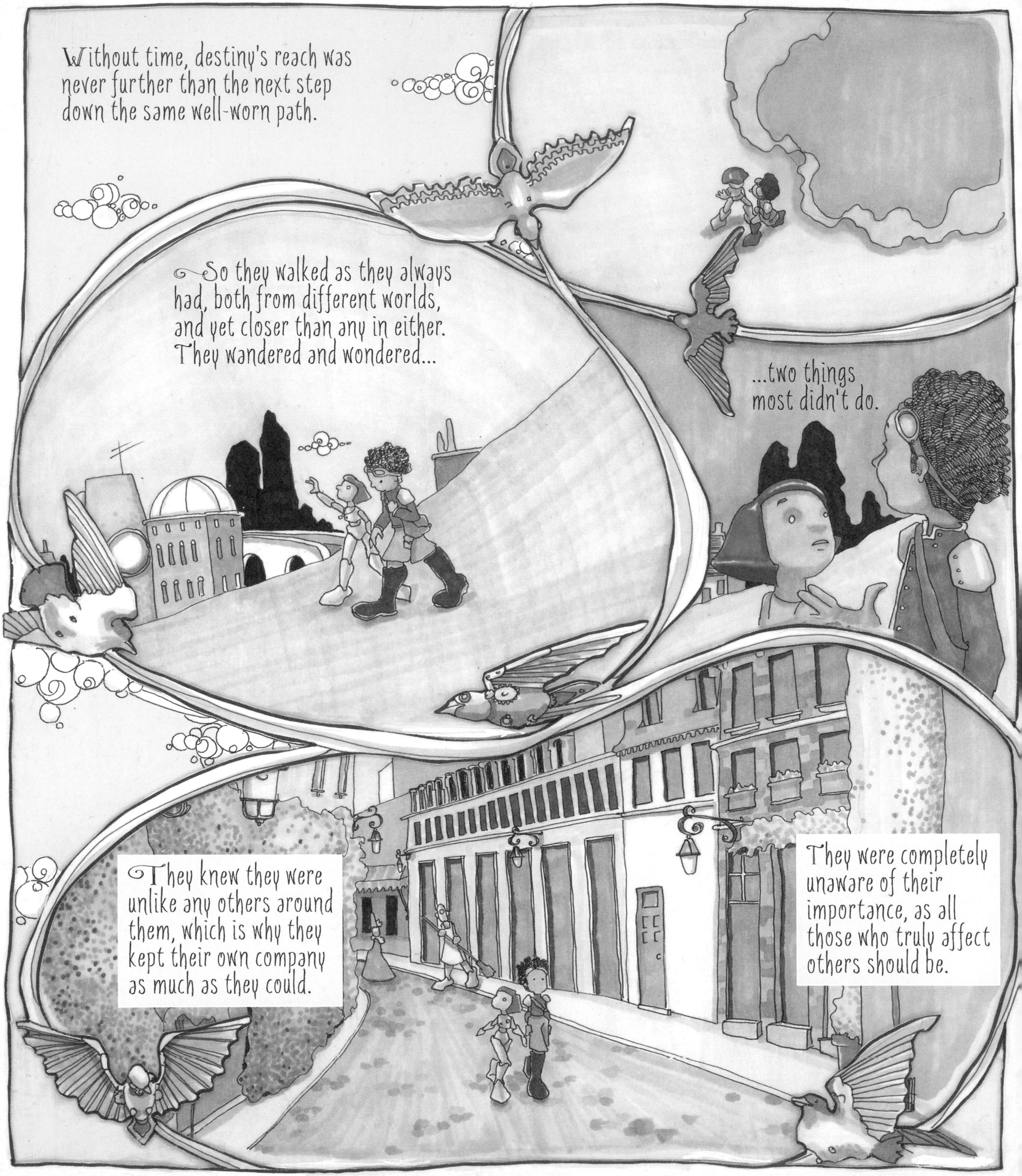
Without time, destiny's reach was never further than the next step down the same well-worn path.
So they walked as they always had, both from different worlds, and yet closer than any in either. They wandered and wondered...
...two things most didn't do.
They knew they were unlike any others around them, which is why they kept their own company as much as they could.
They were completely unaware of their importance, as all those who truly affect others should be.

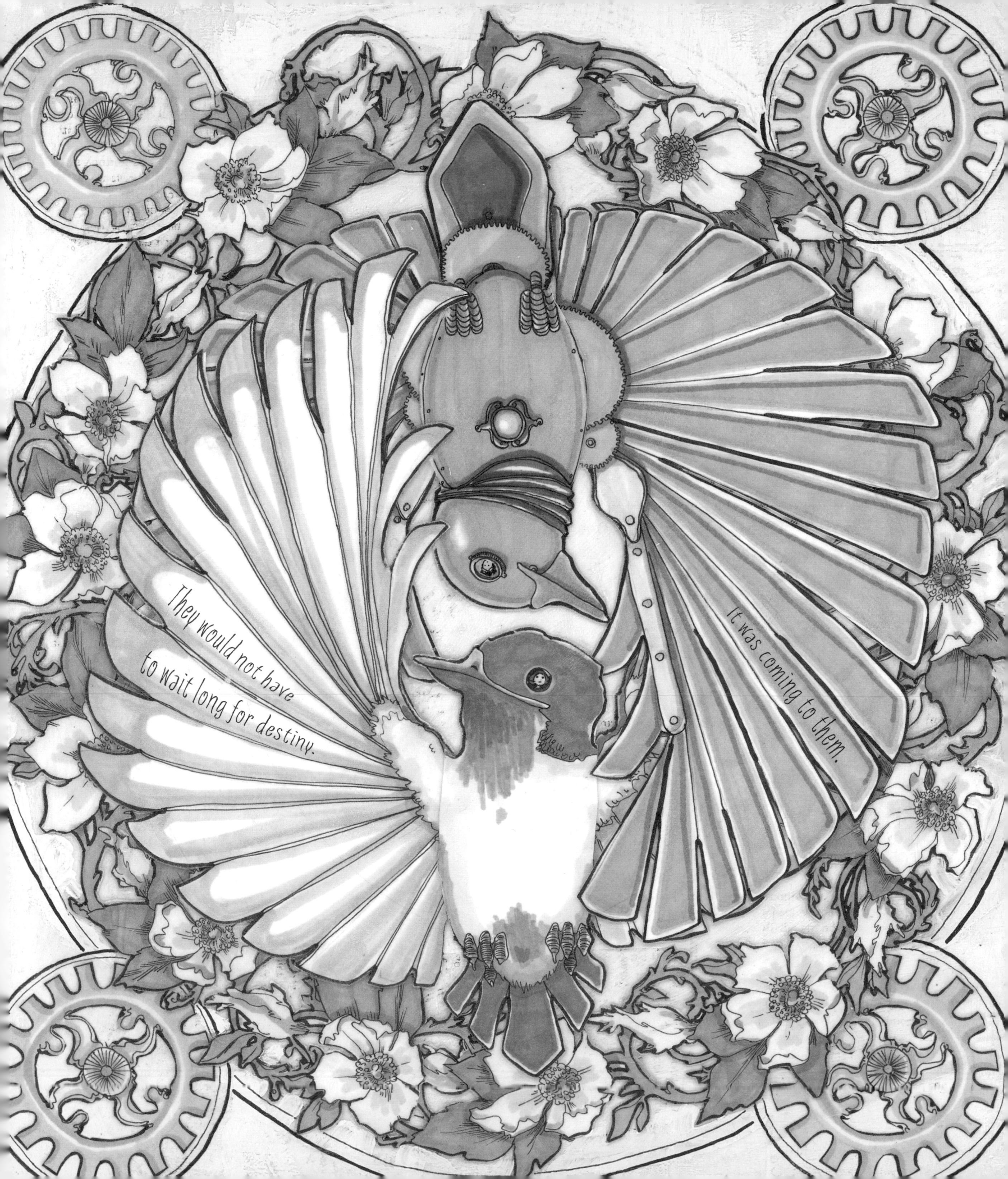
They would not have
to wait long for destiny.
It was coming to them.

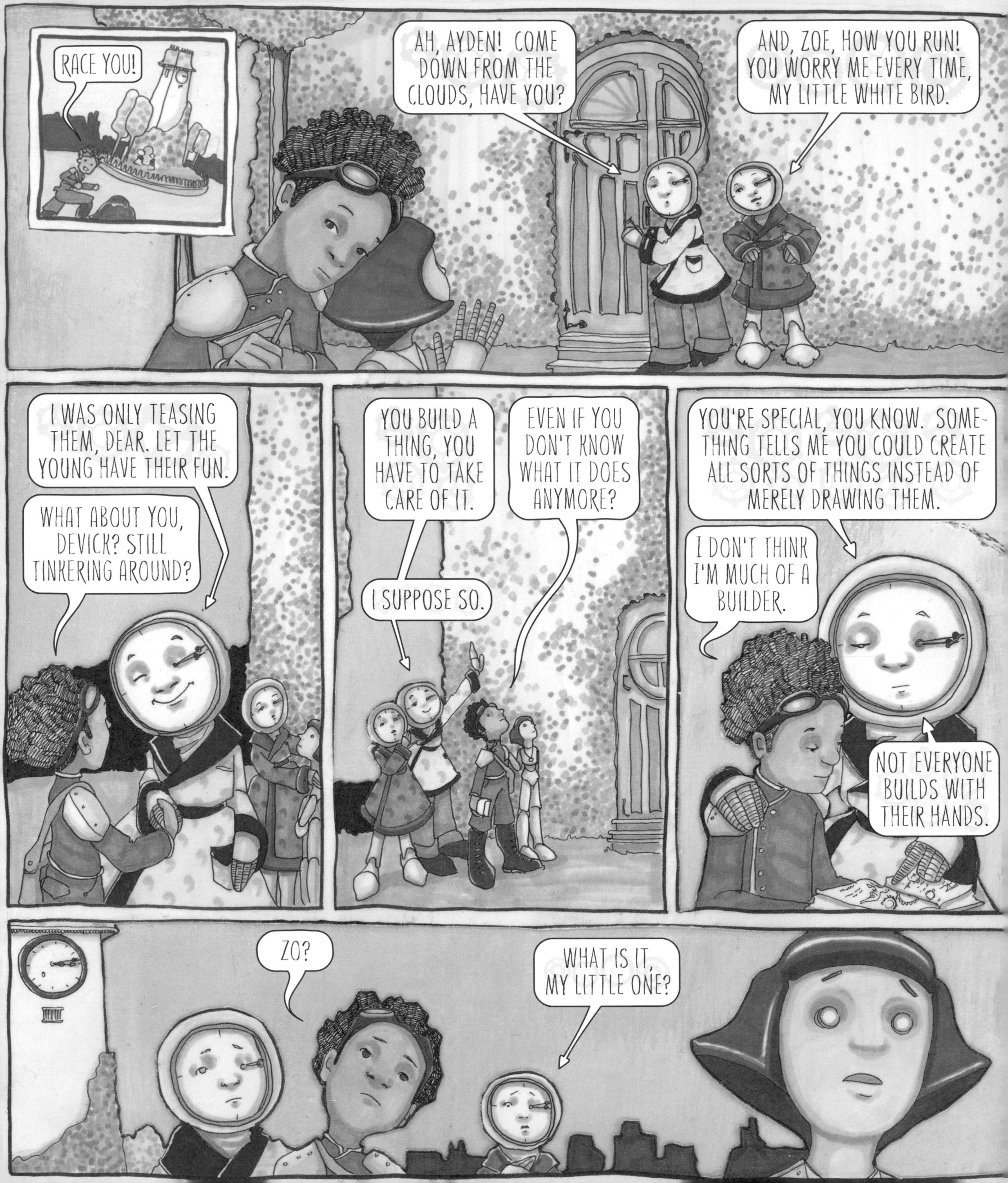
RACE YOU!
AH, AYDEN! COME DOWN FROM THE CLOUDS, HAVE YOU?
AND, ZOE, HOW YOU RUN! YOU WORRY ME EVERY TIME, MY LITTLE WHITE BIRD.
I WAS ONLY TEASING THEM, DEAR. LET THE YOUNG HAVE THEIR FUN.
WHAT ABOUT YOU, DEVICK? STILL TINKERING AROUND?
YOU BUILD A THING, YOU HAVE TO TAKE CARE OF IT.
EVEN IF YOU DON'T KNOW WHAT IT DOES ANYMORE?
I SUPPOSE SO.
YOU'RE SPECIAL, YOU KNOW. SOME-THING TELLS ME YOU COULD CREATE ALL SORTS OF THINGS INSTEAD OF MERELY DRAWING THEM.
I DON'T THINK I'M MUCH OF A BUILDER.
NOT EVERYONE BUILDS WITH THEIR HANDS.
ZO?
WHAT IS IT, MY LITTLE ONE?

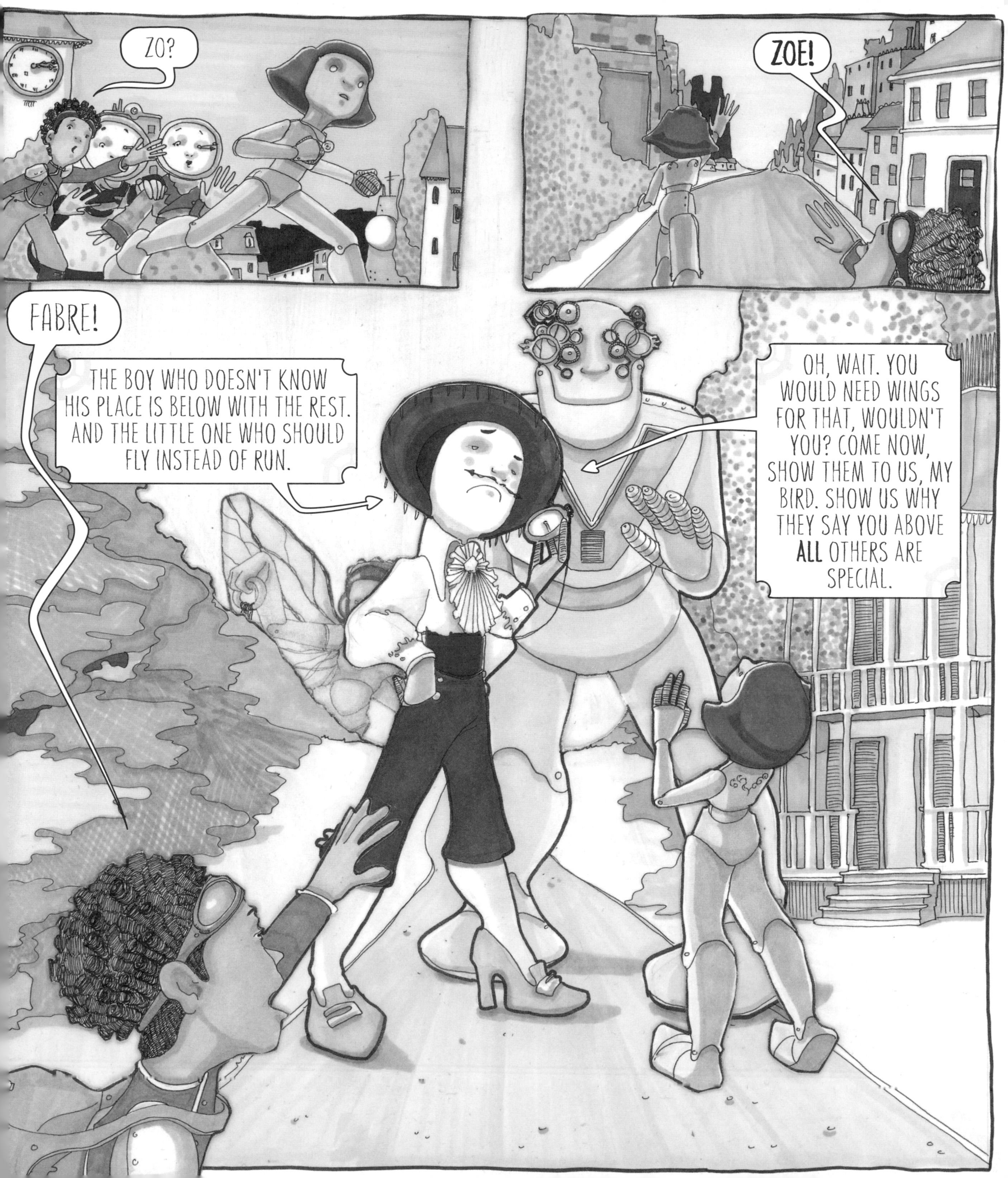
ZO?
ZOE!
FABRE!
THE BOY WHO DOESN'T KNOW HIS PLACE IS BELOW WITH THE REST. AND THE LITTLE ONE WHO SHOULD FLY INSTEAD OF RUN.
OH, WAIT. YOU WOULD NEED WINGS FOR THAT, WOULDN'T YOU? COME NOW, SHOW THEM TO US, MY BIRD. SHOW US WHY THEY SAY YOU ABOVE **ALL** OTHERS ARE SPECIAL.

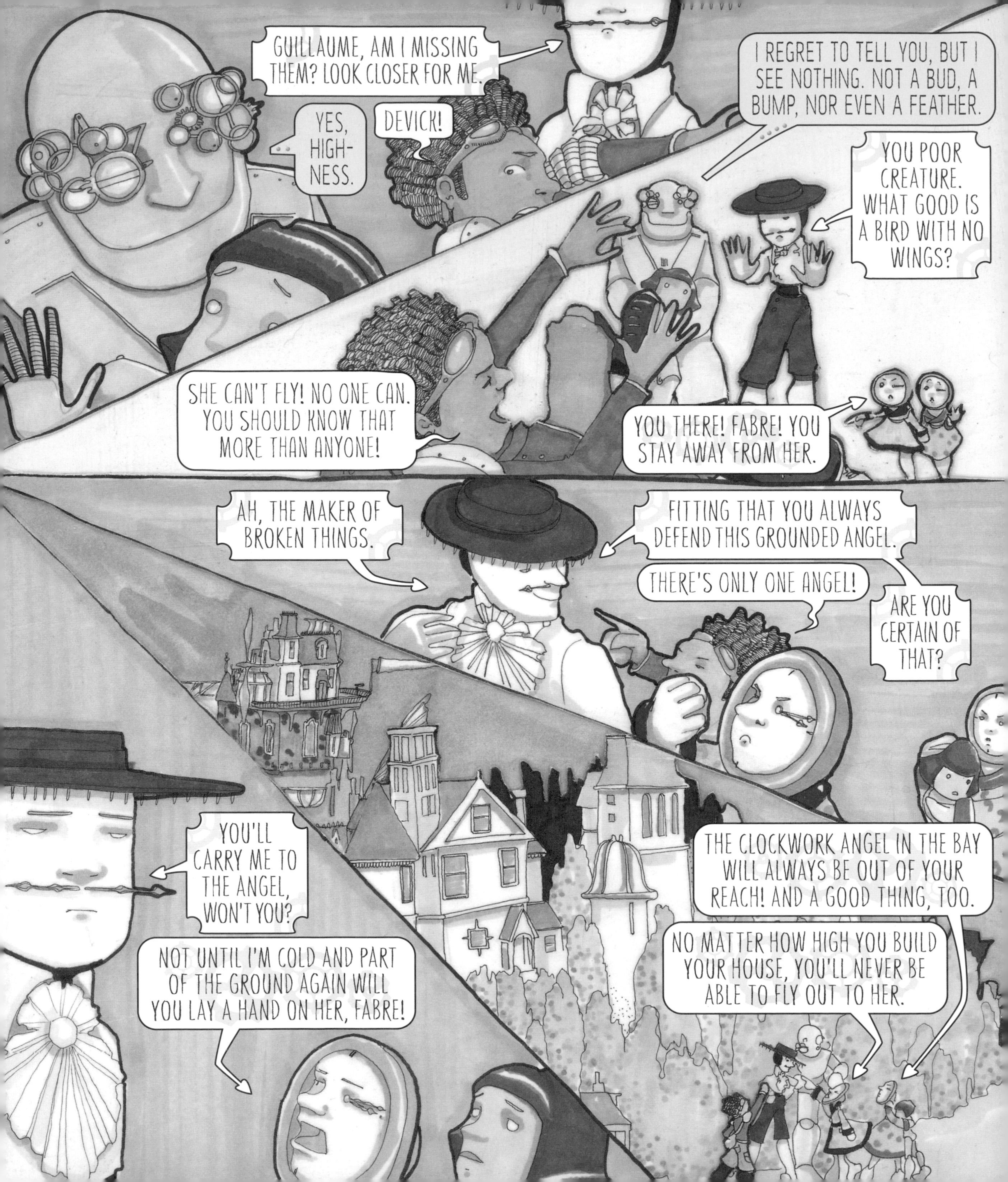
GUILLAUME, AM I MISSING THEM? LOOK CLOSER FOR ME.
YES, HIGH-NESS.
DEVICK!
I REGRET TO TELL YOU, BUT I SEE NOTHING. NOT A BUD, A BUMP, NOR EVEN A FEATHER.
YOU POOR CREATURE. WHAT GOOD IS A BIRD WITH NO WINGS?
SHE CAN'T FLY! NO ONE CAN. YOU SHOULD KNOW THAT MORE THAN ANYONE!
YOU THERE! FABRE! YOU STAY AWAY FROM HER.
AH, THE MAKER OF BROKEN THINGS.
FITTING THAT YOU ALWAYS DEFEND THIS GROUNDED ANGEL.
THERE'S ONLY ONE ANGEL!
ARE YOU CERTAIN OF THAT?
YOU'LL CARRY ME TO THE ANGEL, WON'T YOU?
NOT UNTIL I'M COLD AND PART OF THE GROUND AGAIN WILL YOU LAY A HAND ON HER, FABRE!
THE CLOCKWORK ANGEL IN THE BAY WILL ALWAYS BE OUT OF YOUR REACH! AND A GOOD THING, TOO.
NO MATTER HOW HIGH YOU BUILD YOUR HOUSE, YOU'LL NEVER BE ABLE TO FLY OUT TO HER.

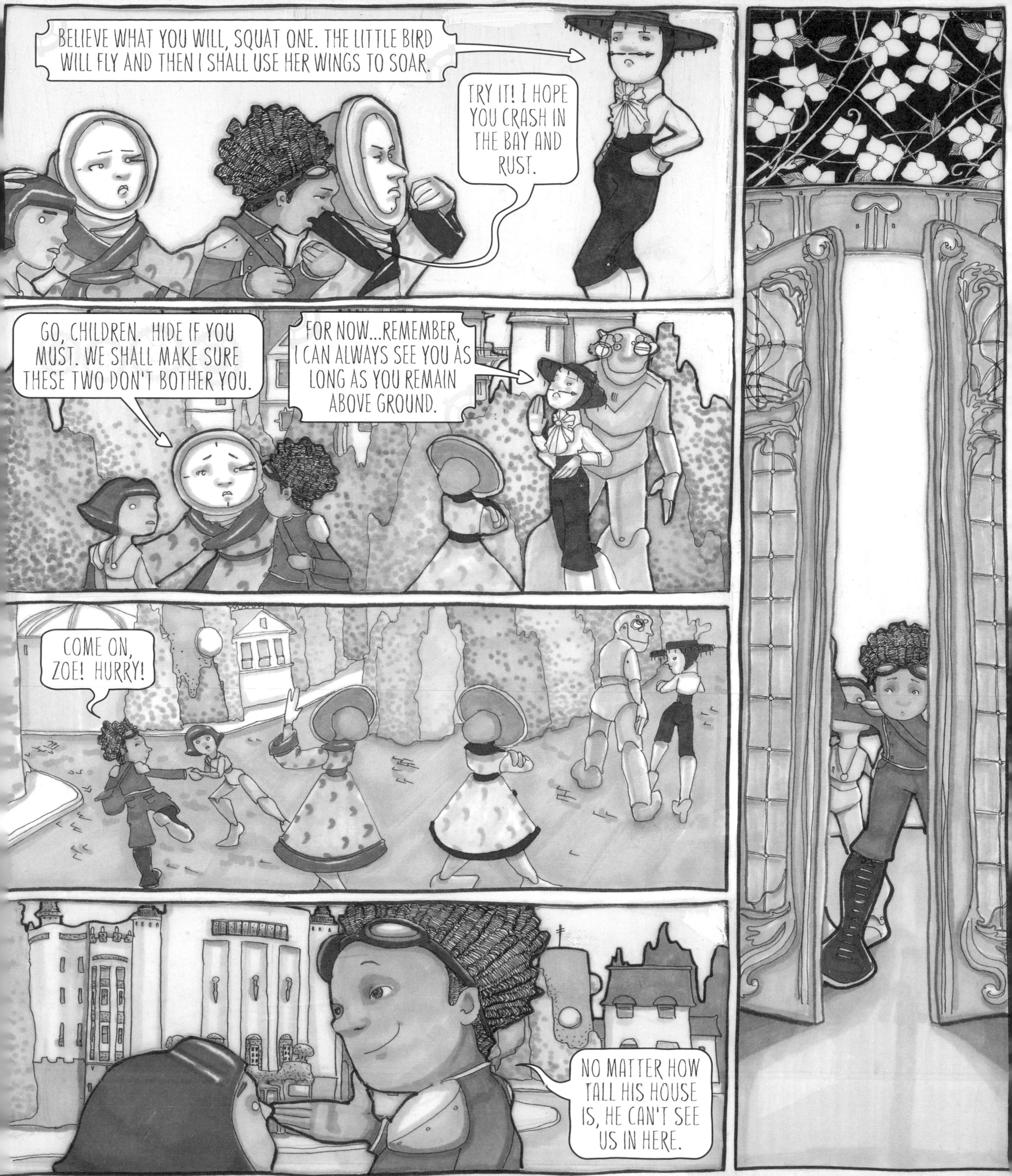
BELIEVE WHAT YOU WILL, SQUAT ONE. THE LITTLE BIRD WILL FLY AND THEN I SHALL USE HER WINGS TO SOAR.
TRY IT! I HOPE YOU CRASH IN THE BAY AND RUST.
GO, CHILDREN. HIDE IF YOU MUST. WE SHALL MAKE SURE THESE TWO DON'T BOTHER YOU.
FOR NOW...REMEMBER, I CAN ALWAYS SEE YOU AS LONG AS YOU REMAIN ABOVE GROUND.
COME ON, ZOE! HURRY!
NO MATTER HOW TALL HIS HOUSE IS, HE CAN'T SEE US IN HERE.

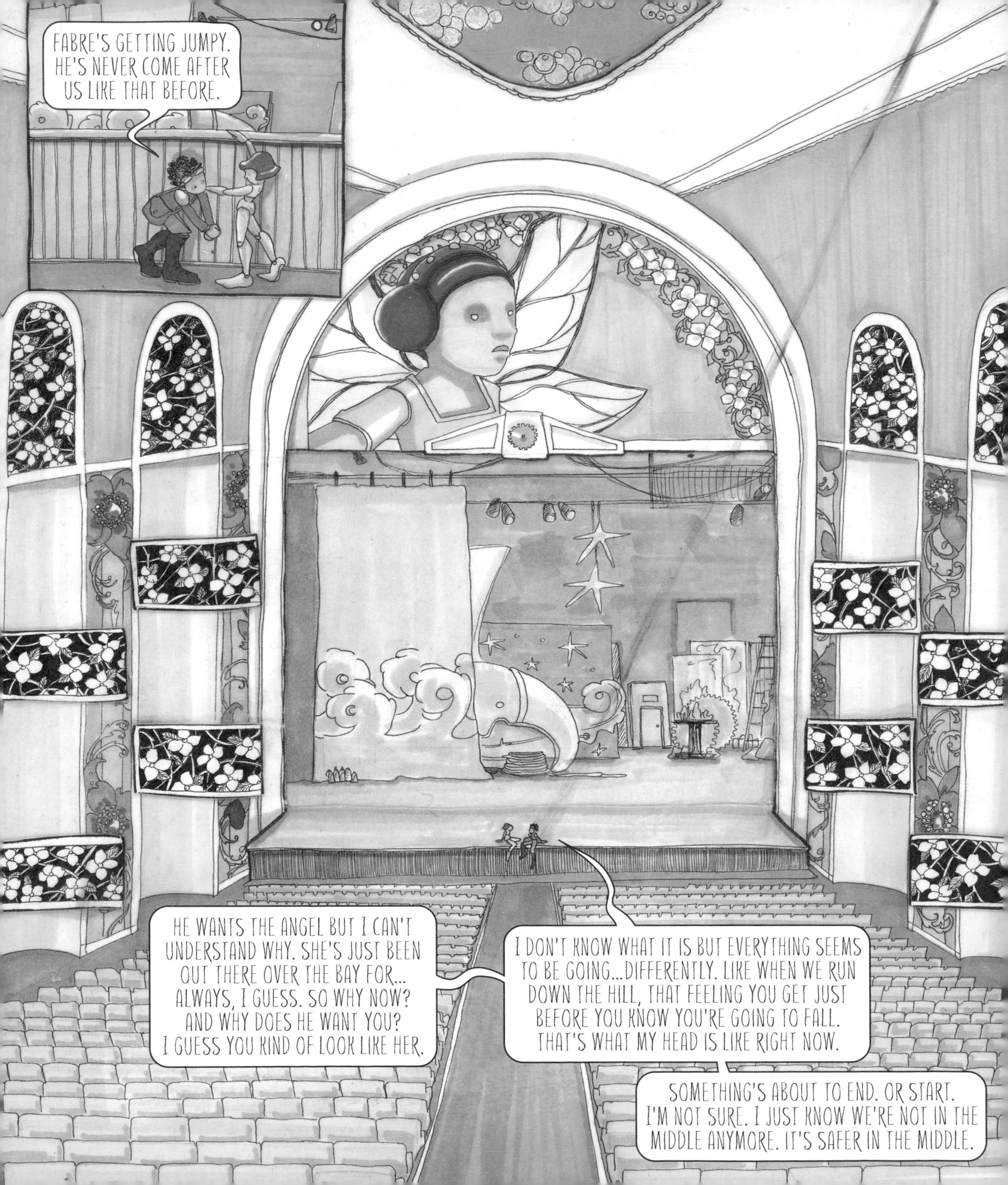
FABRE'S GETTING JUMPY. HE'S NEVER COME AFTER US LIKE THAT BEFORE.
HE WANTS THE ANGEL BUT I CAN'T UNDERSTAND WHY. SHE'S JUST BEEN OUT THERE OVER THE BAY FOR... ALWAYS, I GUESS. SO WHY NOW? AND WHY DOES HE WANT YOU? I GUESS YOU KIND OF LOOK LIKE HER.
I DON'T KNOW WHAT IT IS BUT EVERYTHING SEEMS TO BE GOING...DIFFERENTLY. LIKE WHEN WE RUN DOWN THE HILL, THAT FEELING YOU GET JUST BEFORE YOU KNOW YOU'RE GOING TO FALL. THAT'S WHAT MY HEAD IS LIKE RIGHT NOW.
SOMETHING'S ABOUT TO END. OR START. I'M NOT SURE. I JUST KNOW WE'RE NOT IN THE MIDDLE ANYMORE. IT'S SAFER IN THE MIDDLE.

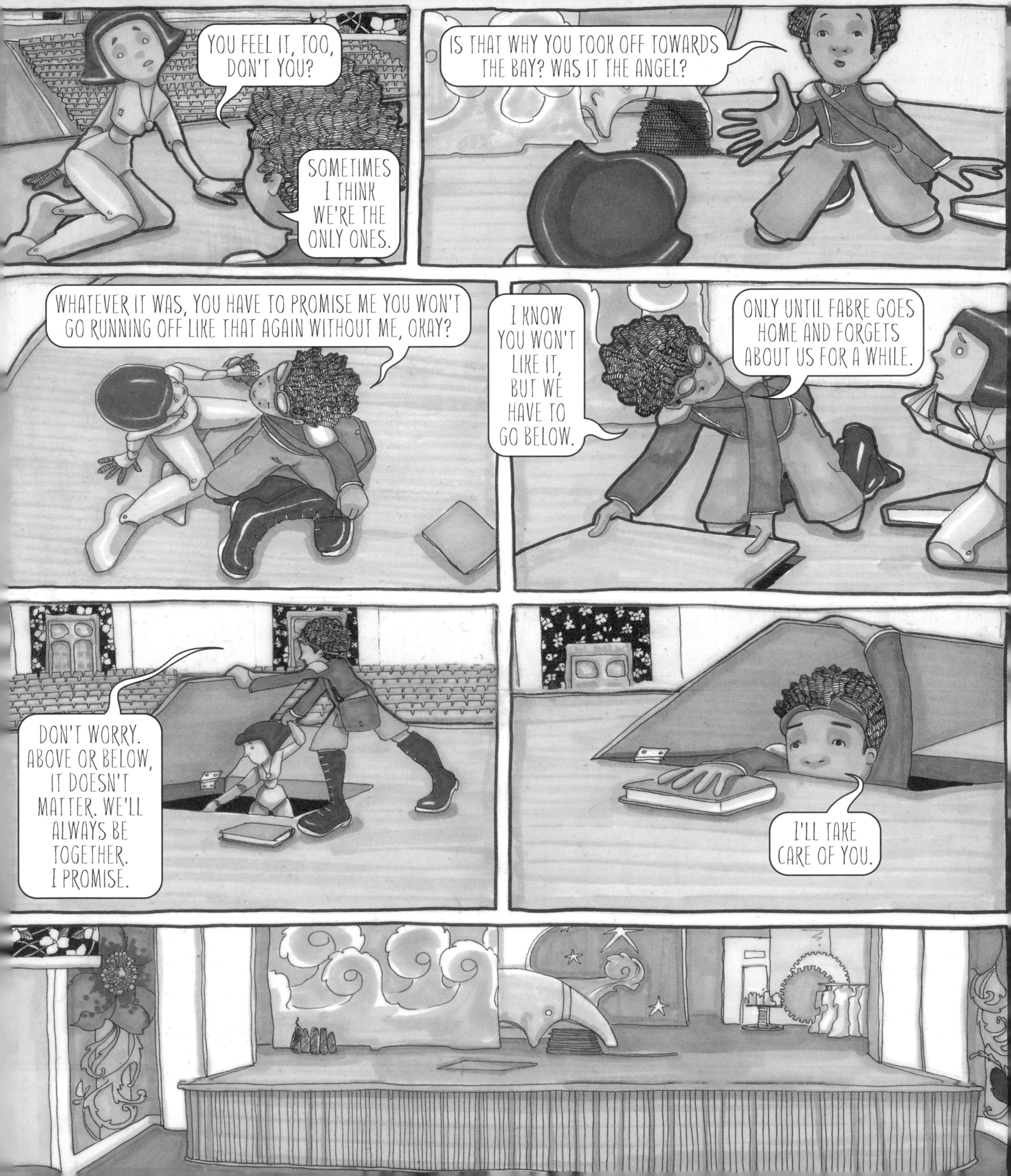
YOU FEEL IT, TOO, DON'T YOU?
SOMETIMES I THINK WE'RE THE ONLY ONES.
IS THAT WHY YOU TOOK OFF TOWARDS THE BAY? WAS IT THE ANGEL?
WHATEVER IT WAS, YOU HAVE TO PROMISE ME YOU WON'T GO RUNNING OFF LIKE THAT AGAIN WITHOUT ME, OKAY?
I KNOW YOU WON'T LIKE IT, BUT WE HAVE TO GO BELOW.
ONLY UNTIL FABRE GOES HOME AND FORGETS ABOUT US FOR A WHILE.
DON'T WORRY. ABOVE OR BELOW, IT DOESN'T MATTER. WE'LL ALWAYS BE TOGETHER. I PROMISE.
I'LL TAKE CARE OF YOU.

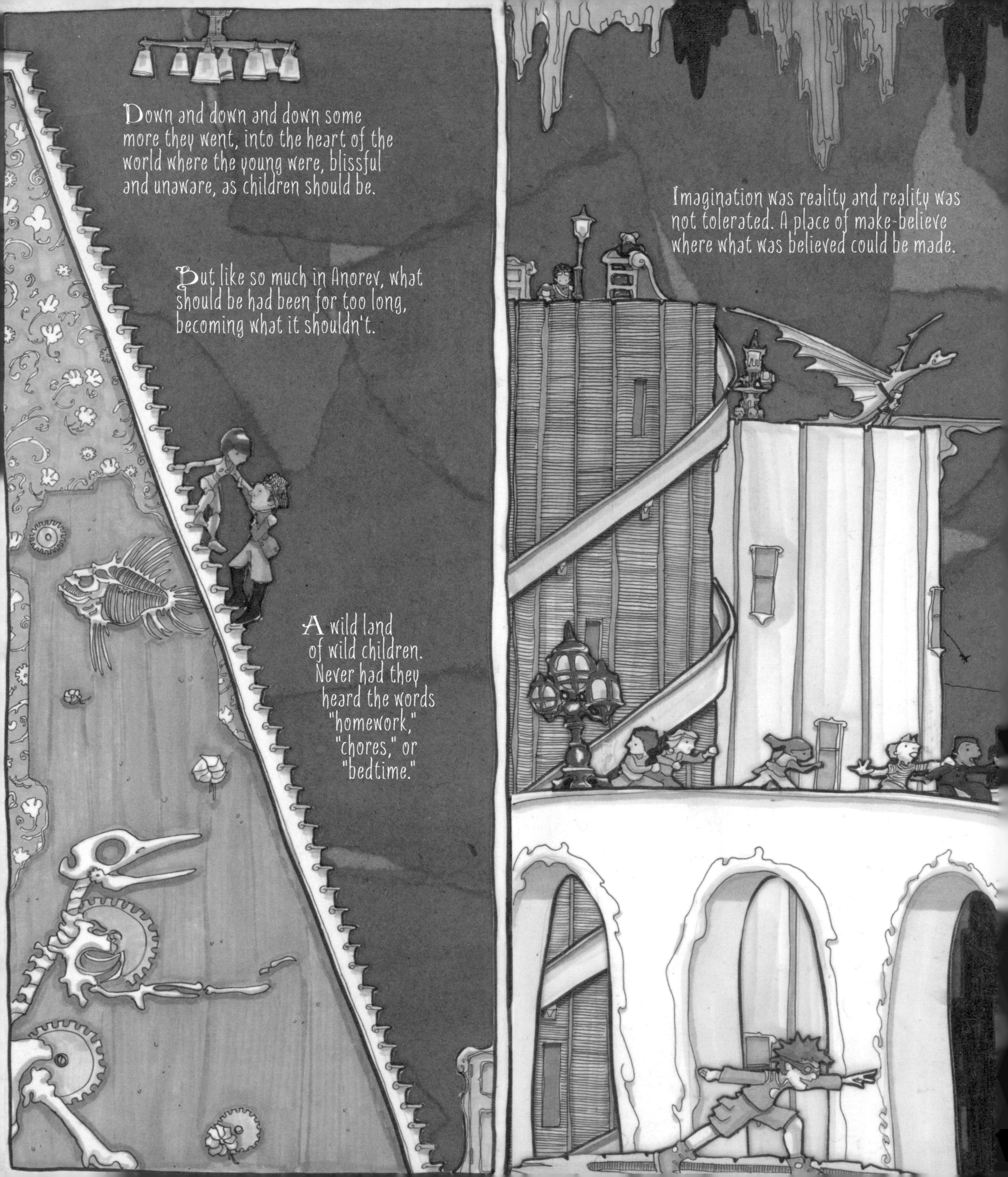
Down and down and down some more they went, into the heart of the world where the young were, blissful and unaware, as children should be.
But like so much in Anorev, what should be had been for too long, becoming what it shouldn't.
A wild land of wild children. Never had they heard the words "homework," "chores," or "bedtime."
Imagination was reality and reality was not tolerated. A place of make-believe where what was believed could be made.

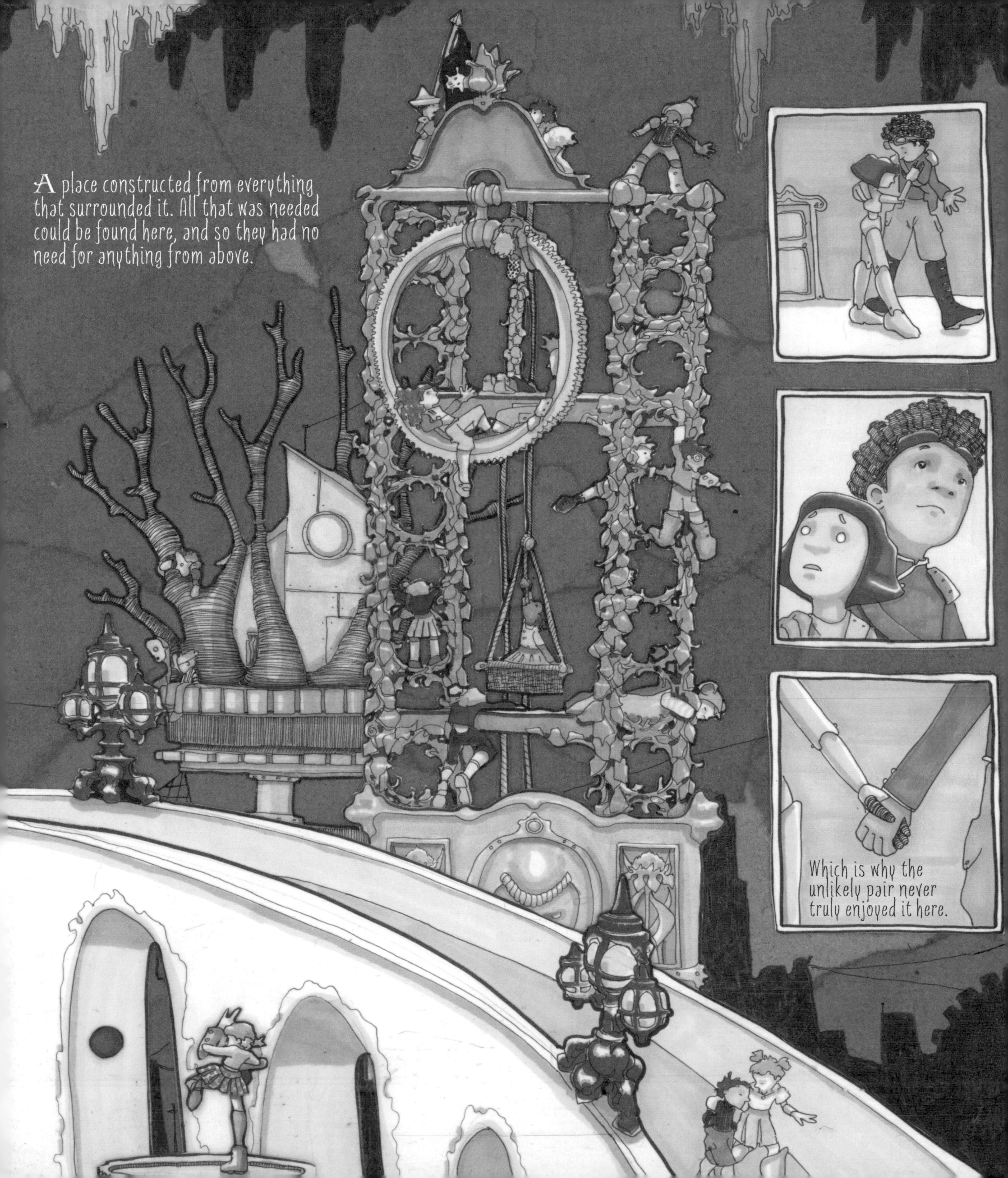
A place constructed from everything that surrounded it. All that was needed could be found here, and so they had no need for anything from above.
Which is why the unlikely pair never truly enjoyed it here.

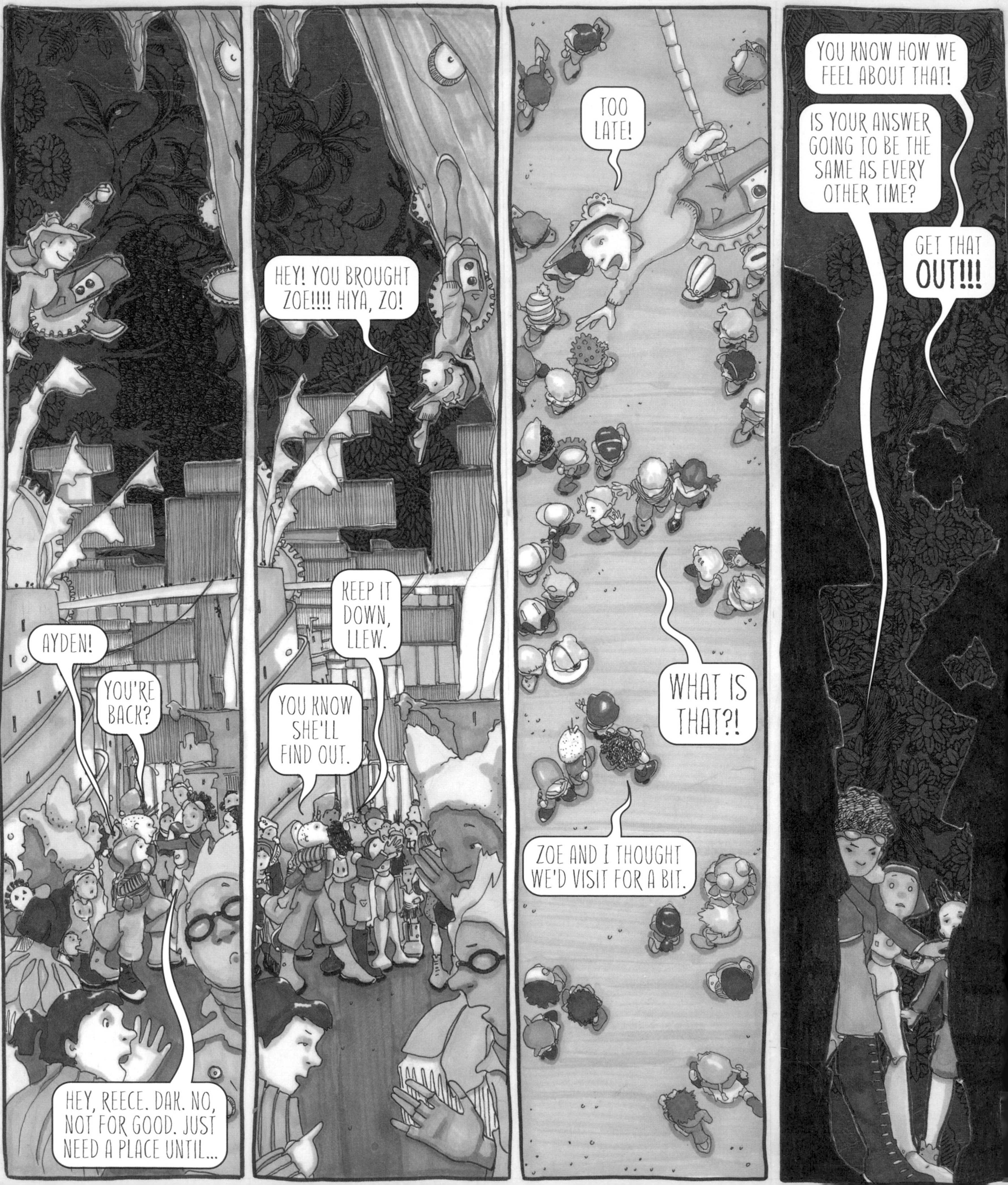
AYDEN!
YOU'RE BACK?
HEY, REECE. DAK. NO, NOT FOR GOOD. JUST NEED A PLACE UNTIL...
HEY! YOU BROUGHT ZOE!!!! HIYA, ZO!
KEEP IT DOWN, LLEW.
YOU KNOW SHE'LL FIND OUT.
TOO LATE!
WHAT IS THAT?!
ZOE AND I THOUGHT WE'D VISIT FOR A BIT.
YOU KNOW HOW WE FEEL ABOUT THAT!
IS YOUR ANSWER GOING TO BE THE SAME AS EVERY OTHER TIME?
GET THAT **OUT!!!**

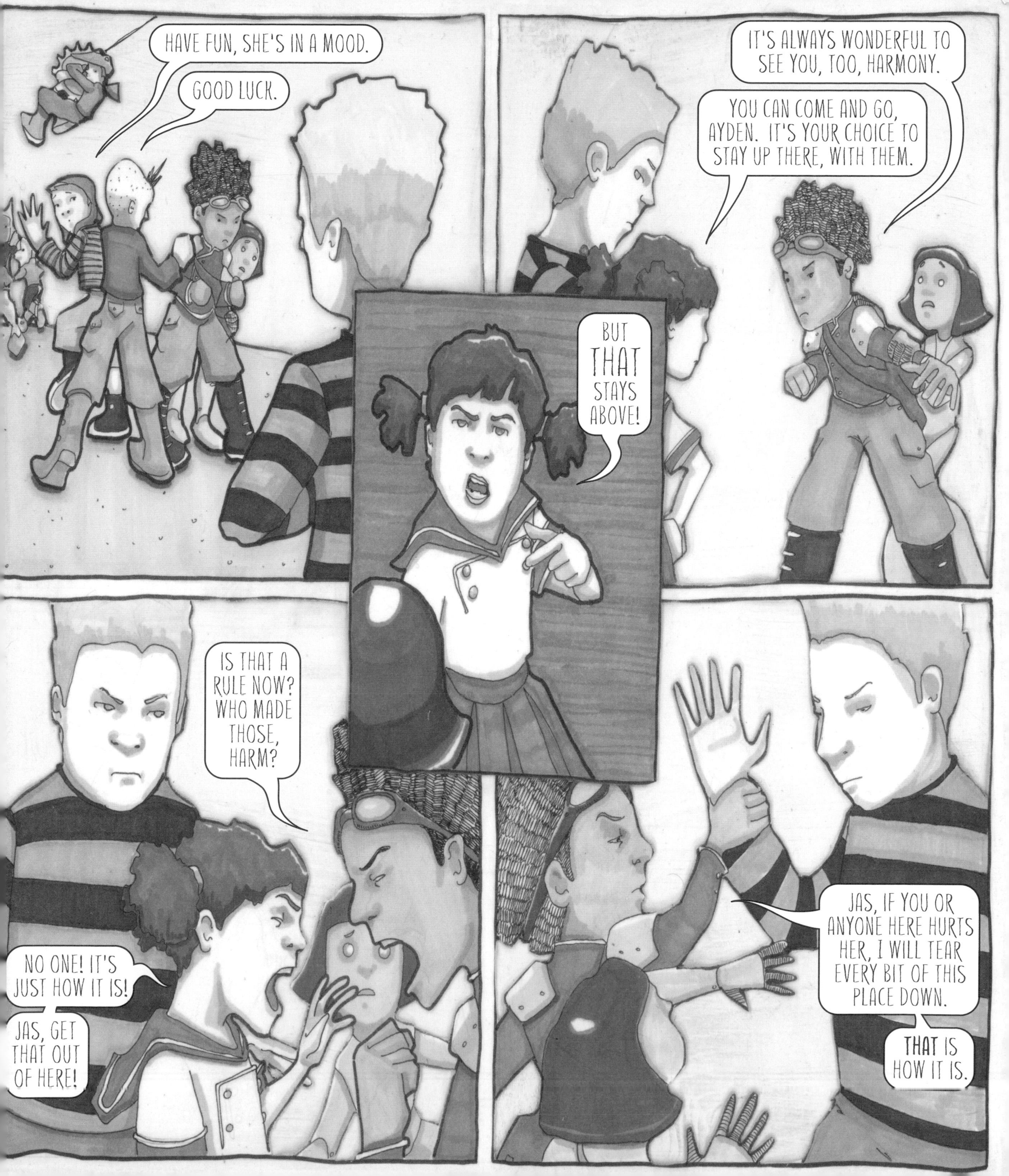
HAVE FUN, SHE'S IN A MOOD.
GOOD LUCK.
IT'S ALWAYS WONDERFUL TO SEE YOU, TOO, HARMONY.
YOU CAN COME AND GO, AYDEN. IT'S YOUR CHOICE TO STAY UP THERE, WITH THEM.
BUT THAT STAYS ABOVE!
IS THAT A RULE NOW? WHO MADE THOSE, HARM?
NO ONE! IT'S JUST HOW IT IS!
JAS, GET THAT OUT OF HERE!
JAS, IF YOU OR ANYONE HERE HURTS HER, I WILL TEAR EVERY BIT OF THIS PLACE DOWN.
THAT IS HOW IT IS.

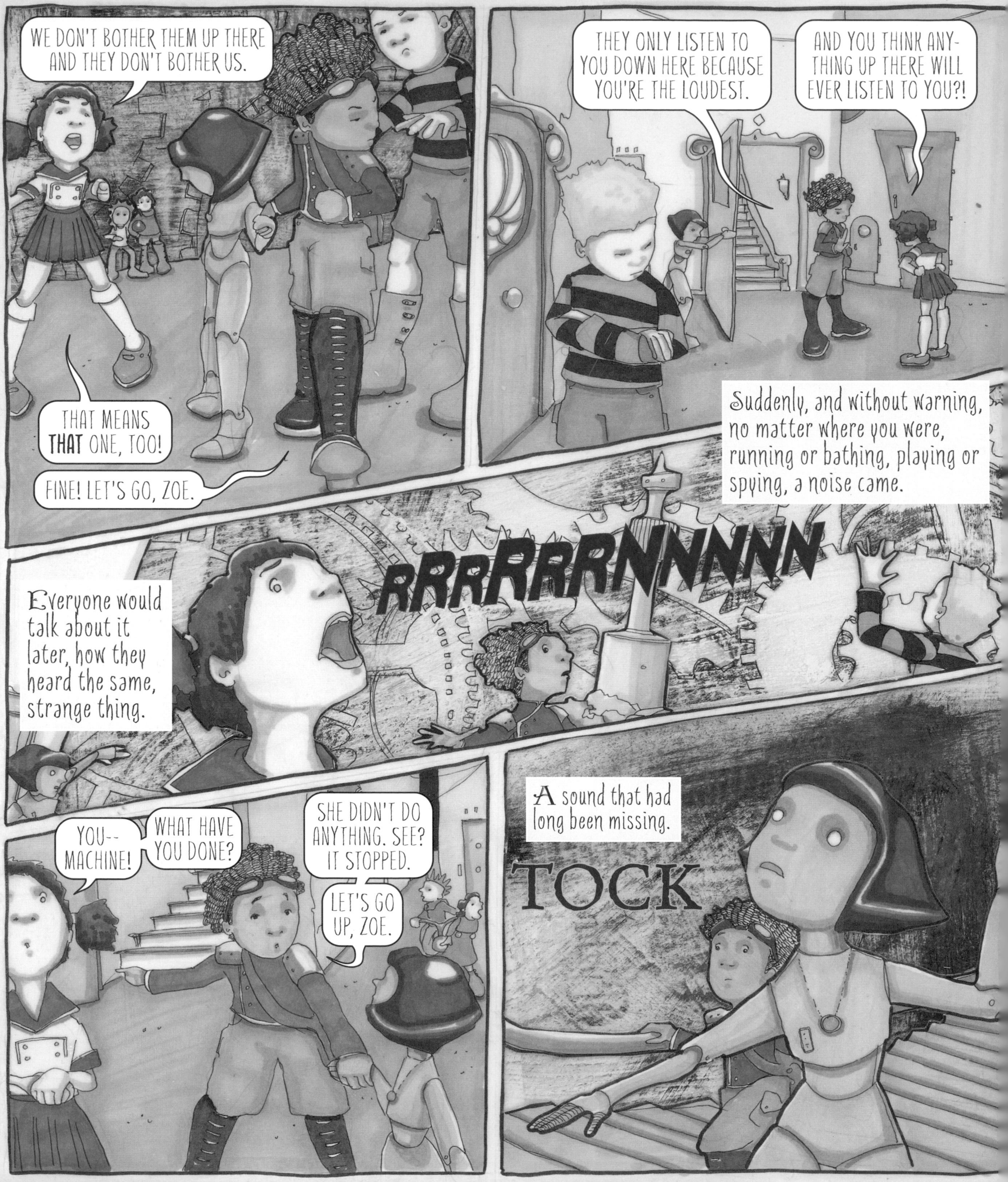

WE DON'T BOTHER THEM UP THERE AND THEY DON'T BOTHER US.
THAT MEANS **THAT** ONE, TOO!
FINE! LET'S GO, ZOE.
THEY ONLY LISTEN TO YOU DOWN HERE BECAUSE YOU'RE THE LOUDEST.
AND YOU THINK ANY-THING UP THERE WILL EVER LISTEN TO YOU?!
Suddenly, and without warning, no matter where you were, running or bathing, playing or spying, a noise came.
Everyone would talk about it later, how they heard the same, strange thing.
RRRRRRNNNNNN
YOU-- MACHINE!
WHAT HAVE YOU DONE?
SHE DIDN'T DO ANYTHING. SEE? IT STOPPED.
LET'S GO UP, ZOE.
A sound that had long been missing.
TOCK

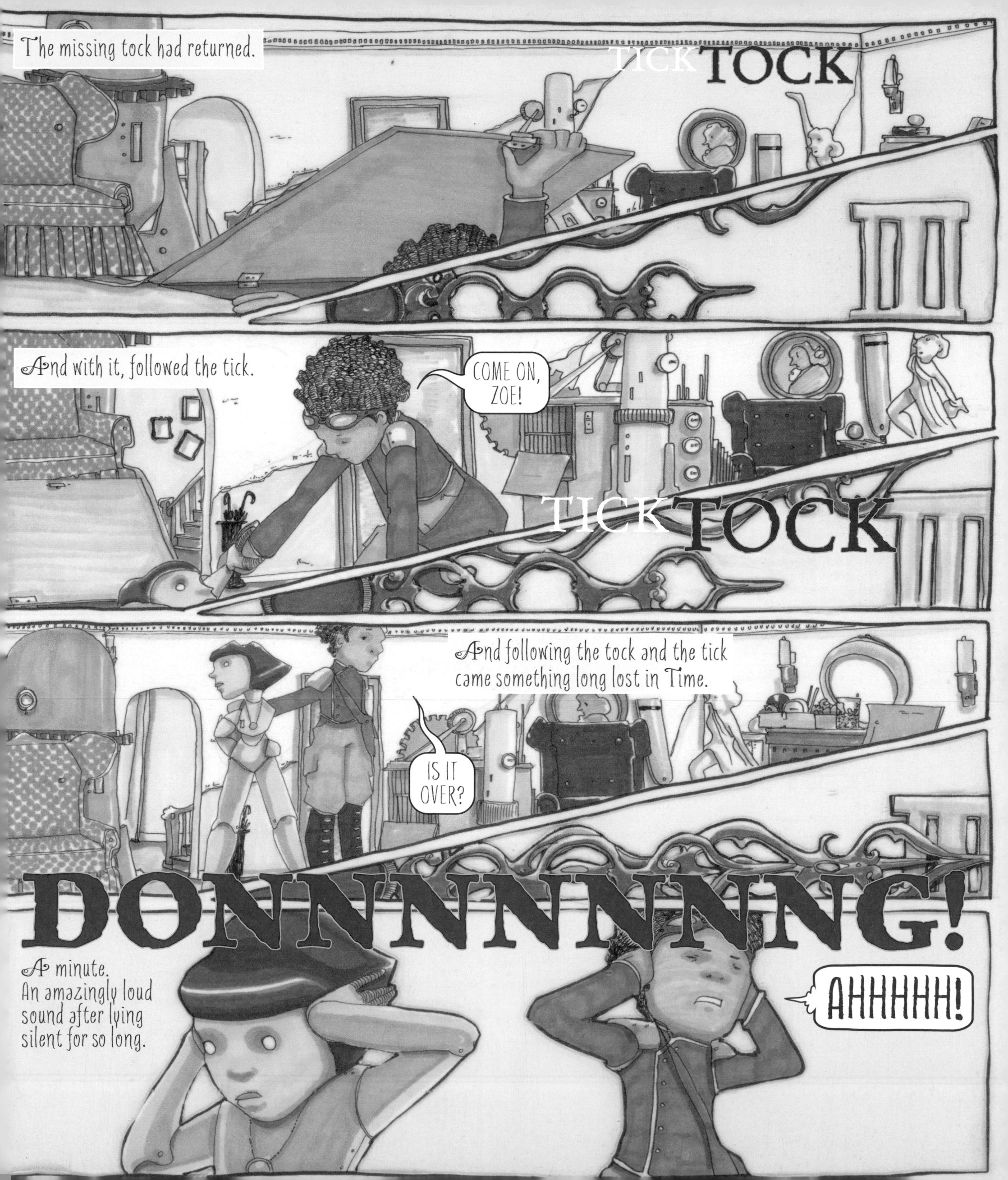
The missing tock had returned.
TICK TOCK
And with it, followed the tick.
COME ON, ZOE!
TICK TOCK
And following the tock and the tick came something long lost in Time.
IS IT OVER?
DONNNNNNNG!
A minute. An amazingly loud sound after lying silent for so long.
AHHHHH!

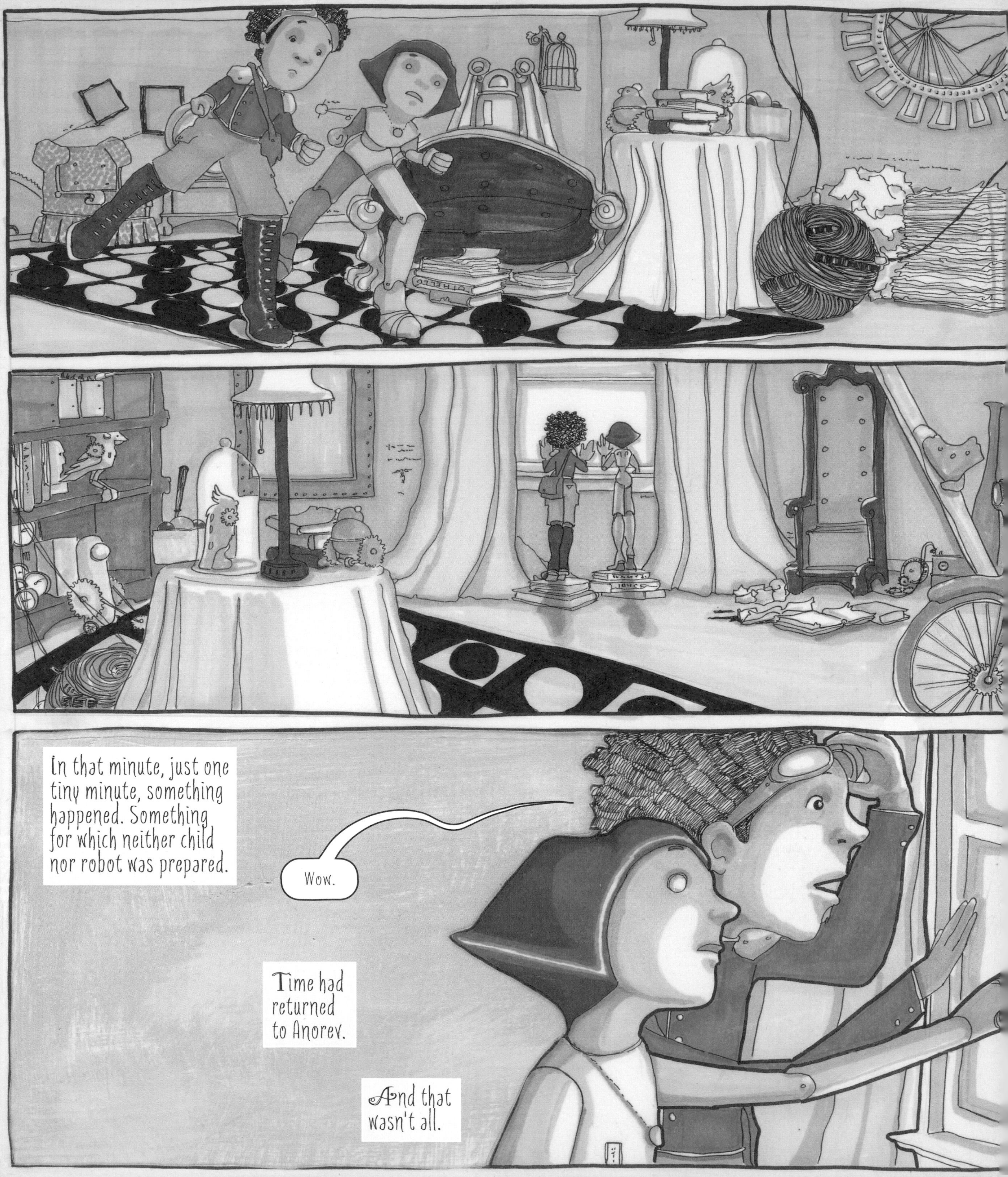

OTHELLO
JOYCE
In that minute, just one tiny minute, something happened. Something for which neither child nor robot was prepared.
Wow.
Time had returned to Anorev.
And that wasn't all.

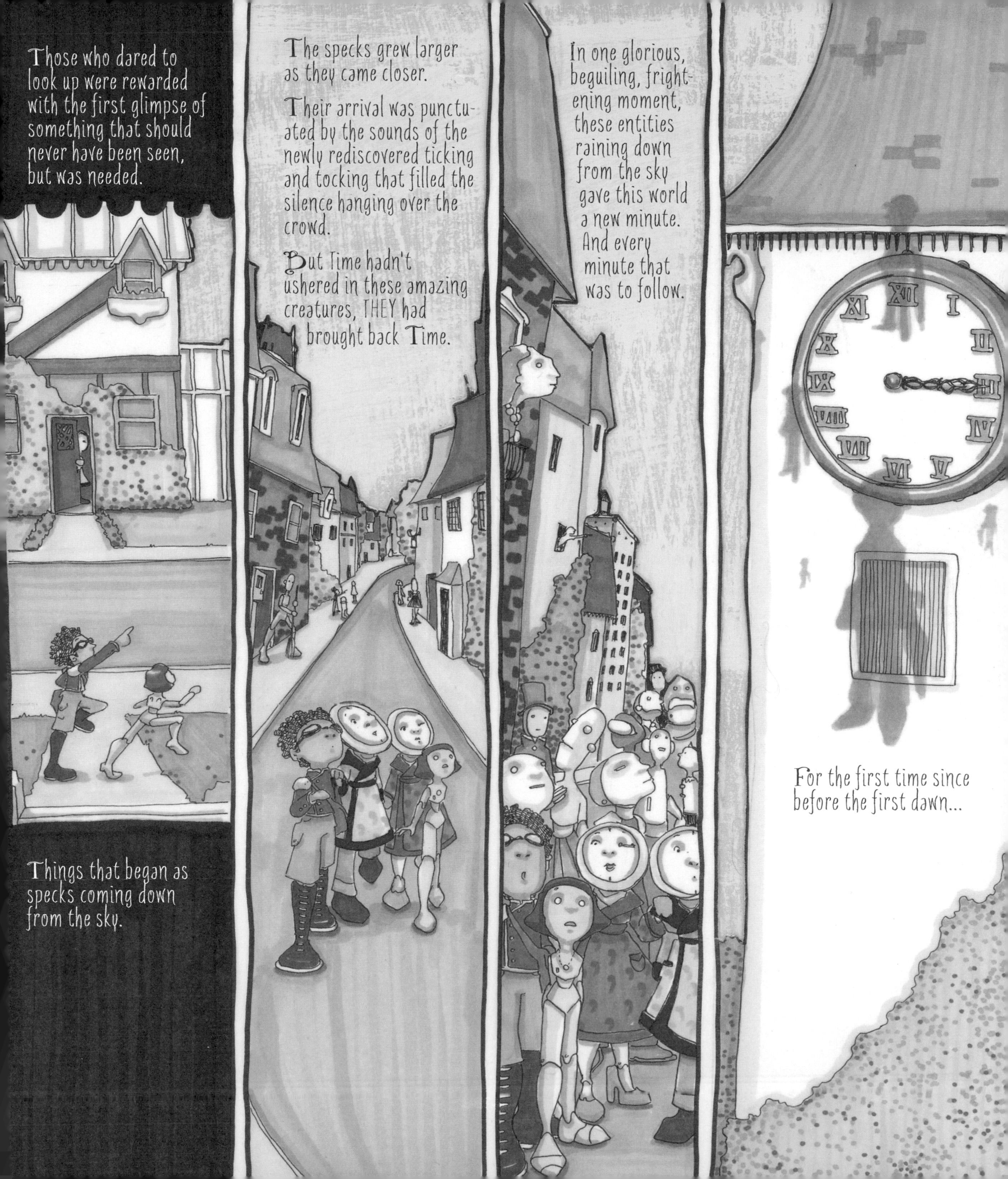
Those who dared to look up were rewarded with the first glimpse of something that should never have been seen, but was needed.
Things that began as specks coming down from the sky.
The specks grew larger as they came closer.
Their arrival was punctuated by the sounds of the newly rediscovered ticking and tocking that filled the silence hanging over the crowd.
But Time hadn't ushered in these amazing creatures, THEY had brought back Time.
In one glorious, beguiling, frightening moment, these entities raining down from the sky gave this world a new minute. And every minute that was to follow.
For the first time since before the first dawn...

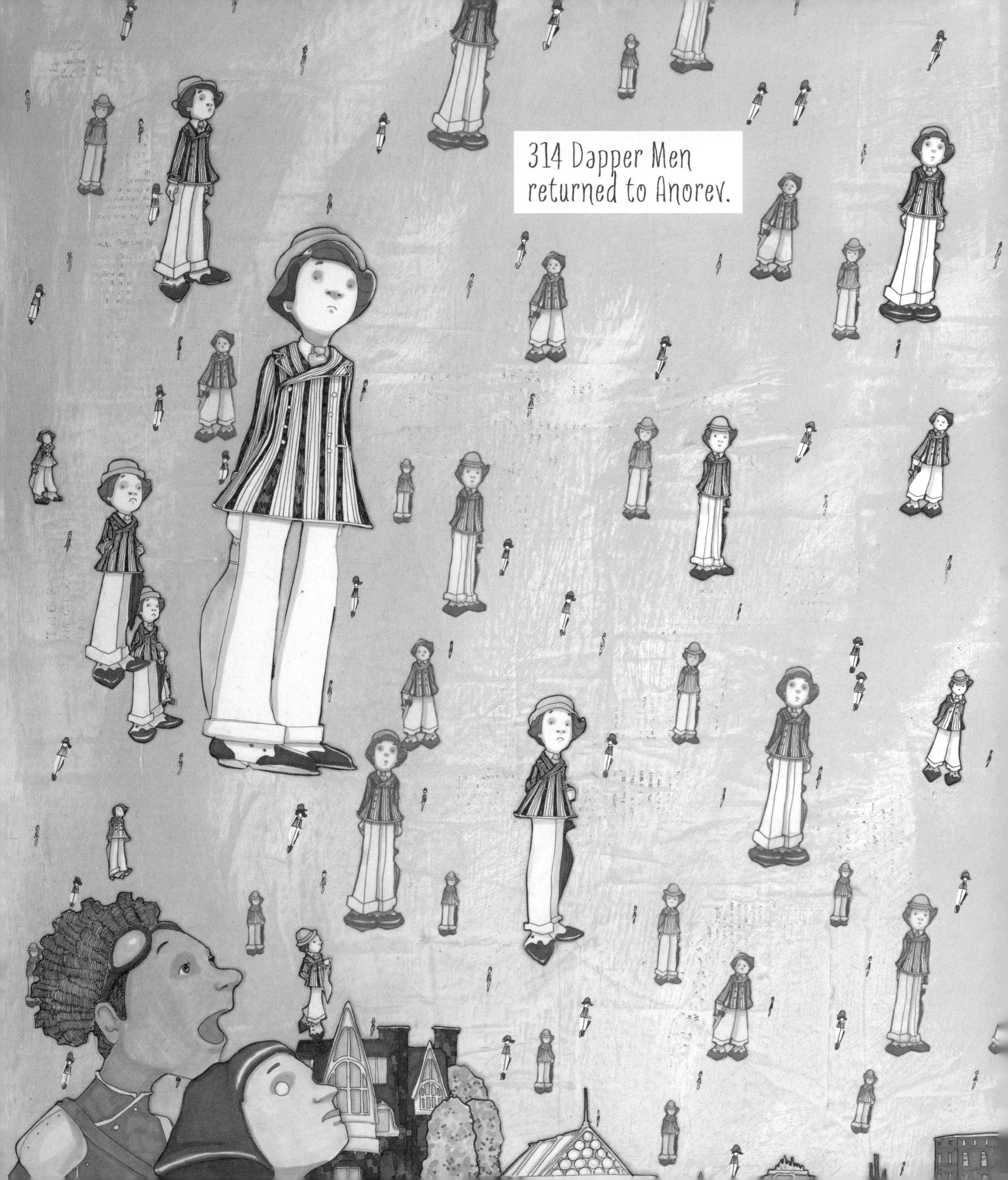
314 Dapper Men returned to Anorev.

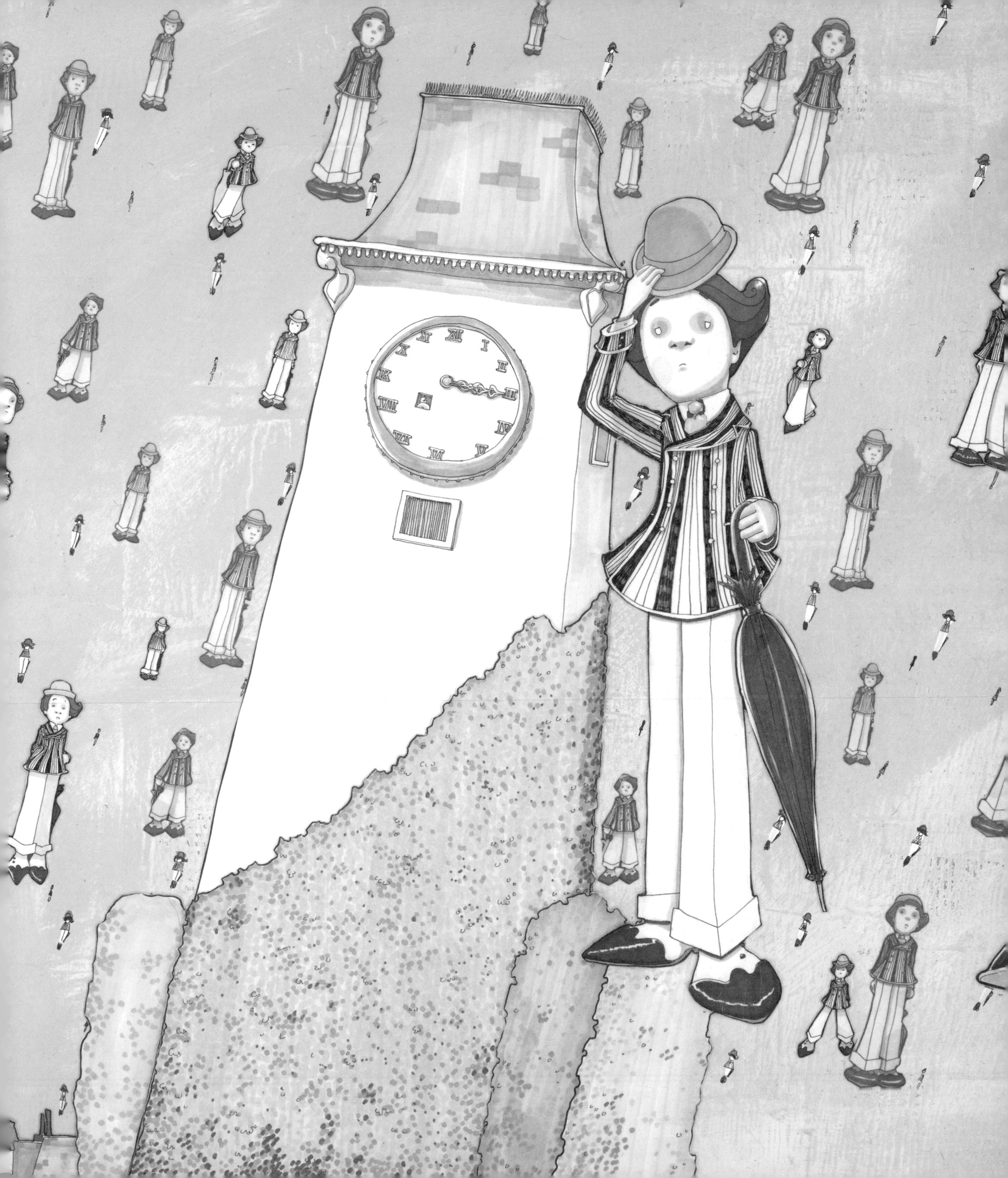

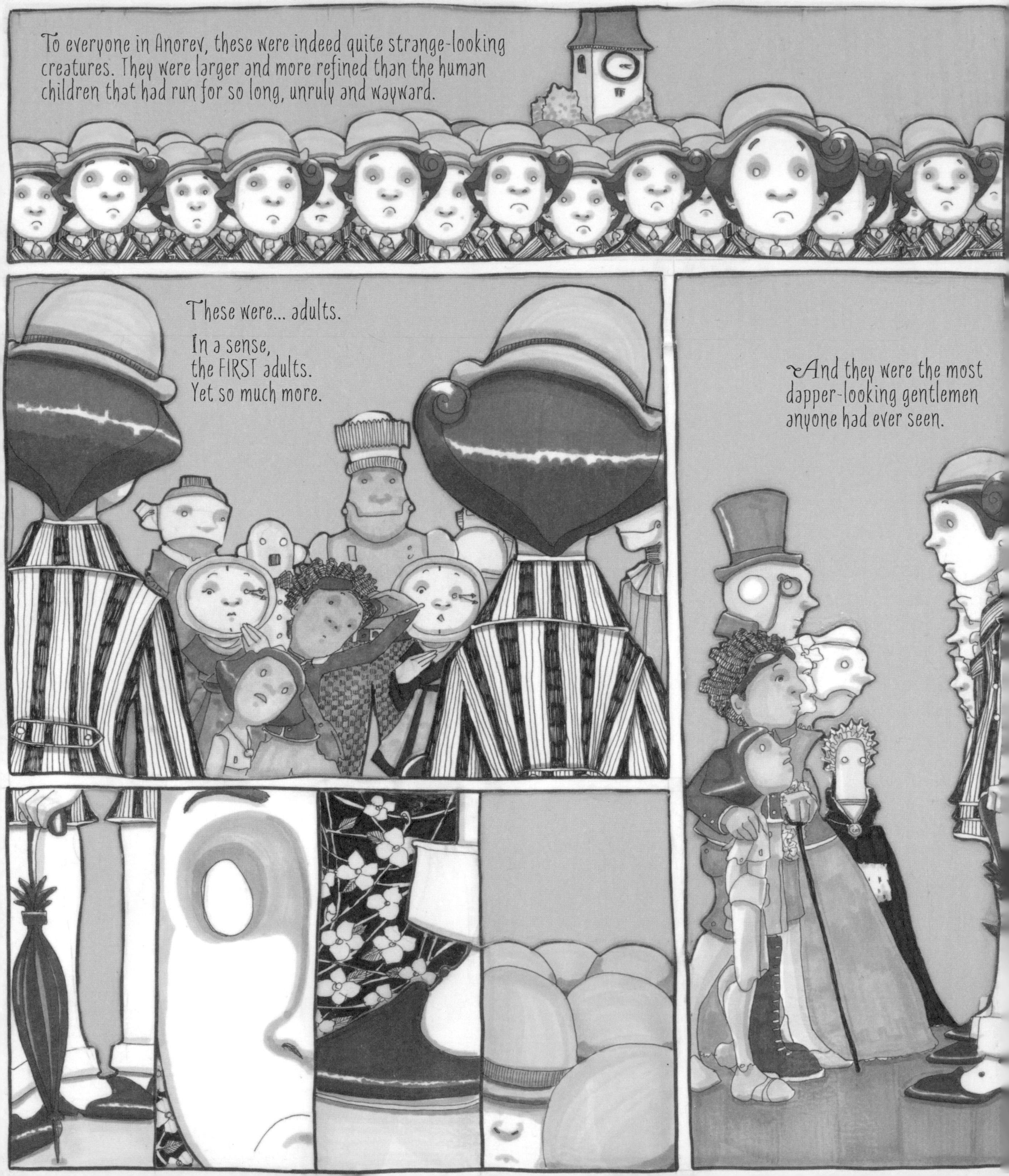
To everyone in Anorev, these were indeed quite strange-looking creatures. They were larger and more refined than the human children that had run for so long, unruly and wayward.
These were... adults.
In a sense, the FIRST adults. Yet so much more.
And they were the most dapper-looking gentlemen anyone had ever seen.

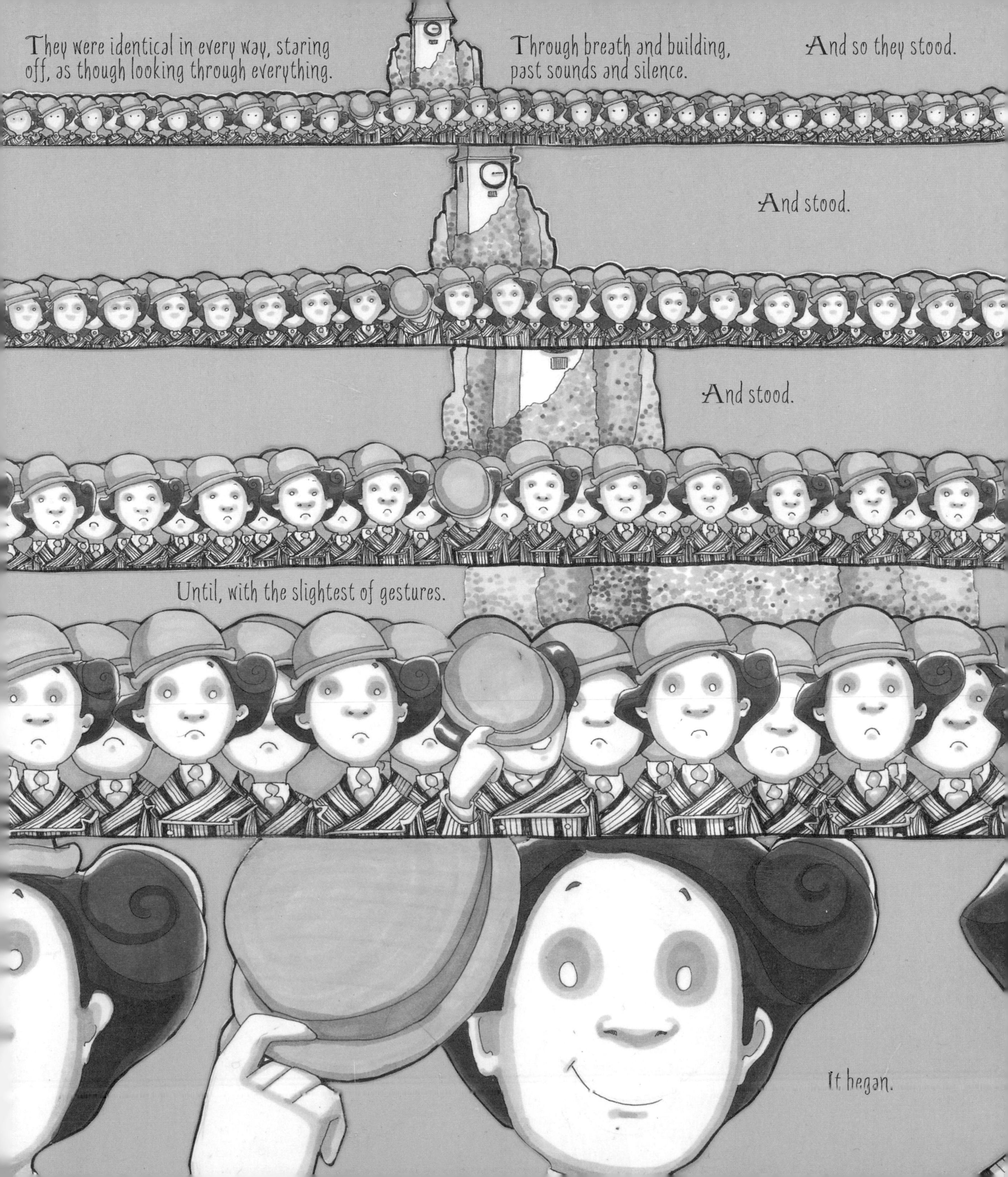
They were identical in every way, staring off, as though looking through everything.
Through breath and building, past sounds and silence.
And so they stood.
And stood.
And stood.
Until, with the slightest of gestures.
It began.

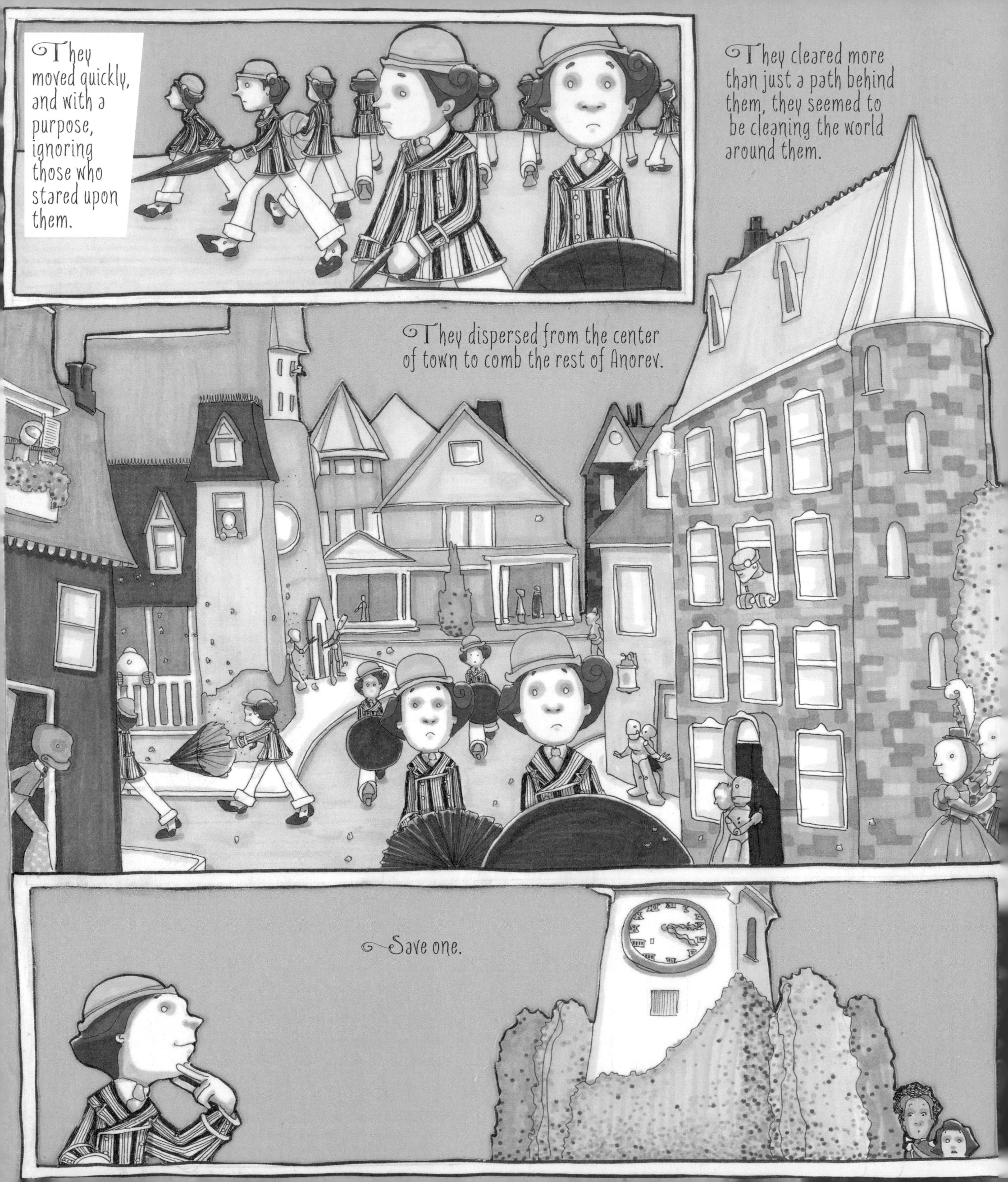

They moved quickly, and with a purpose, ignoring those who stared upon them.
They cleared more than just a path behind them, they seemed to be cleaning the world around them.
They dispersed from the center of town to comb the rest of Anorev.
Save one.

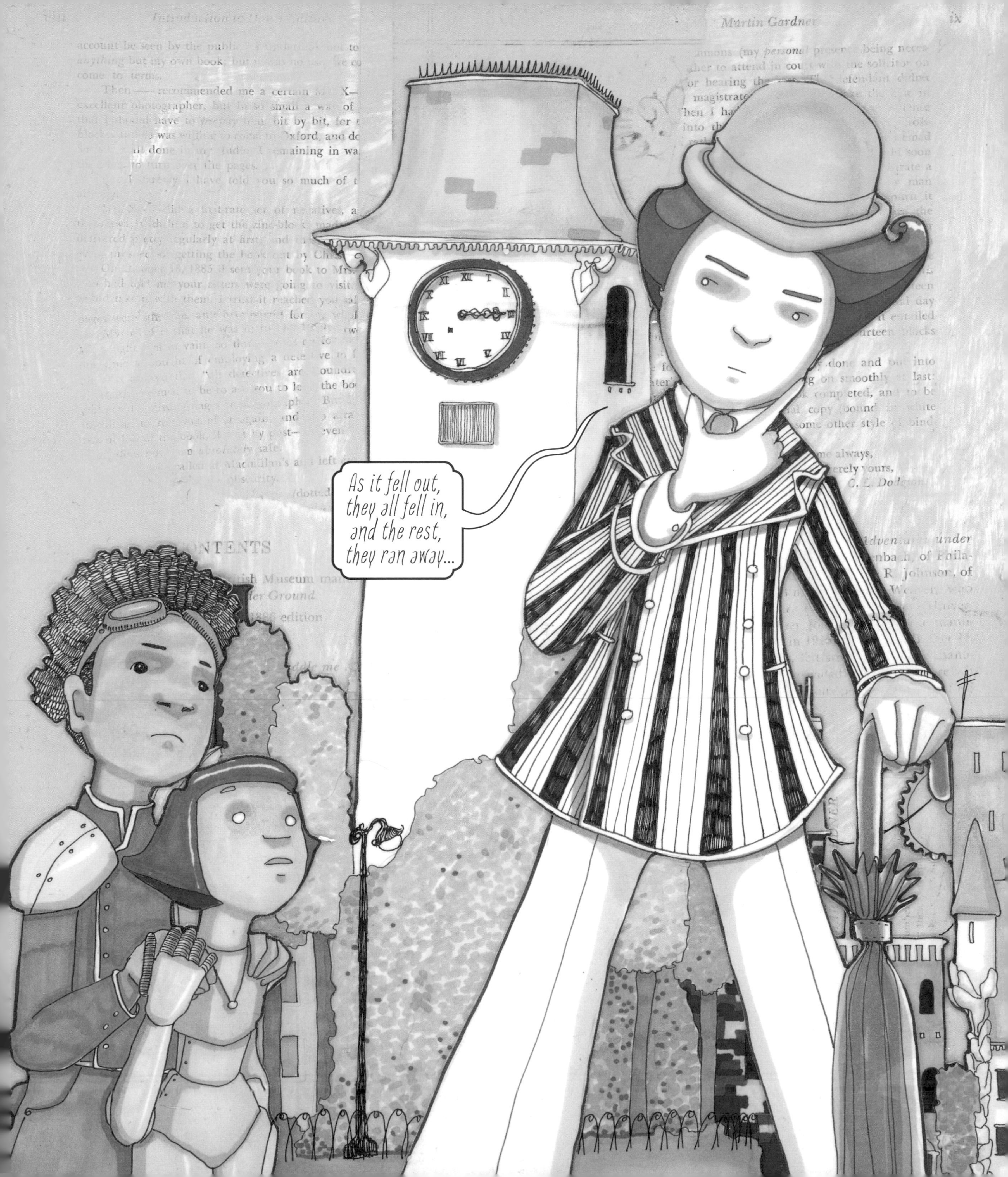
As it fell out, they all fell in, and the rest, they ran away...

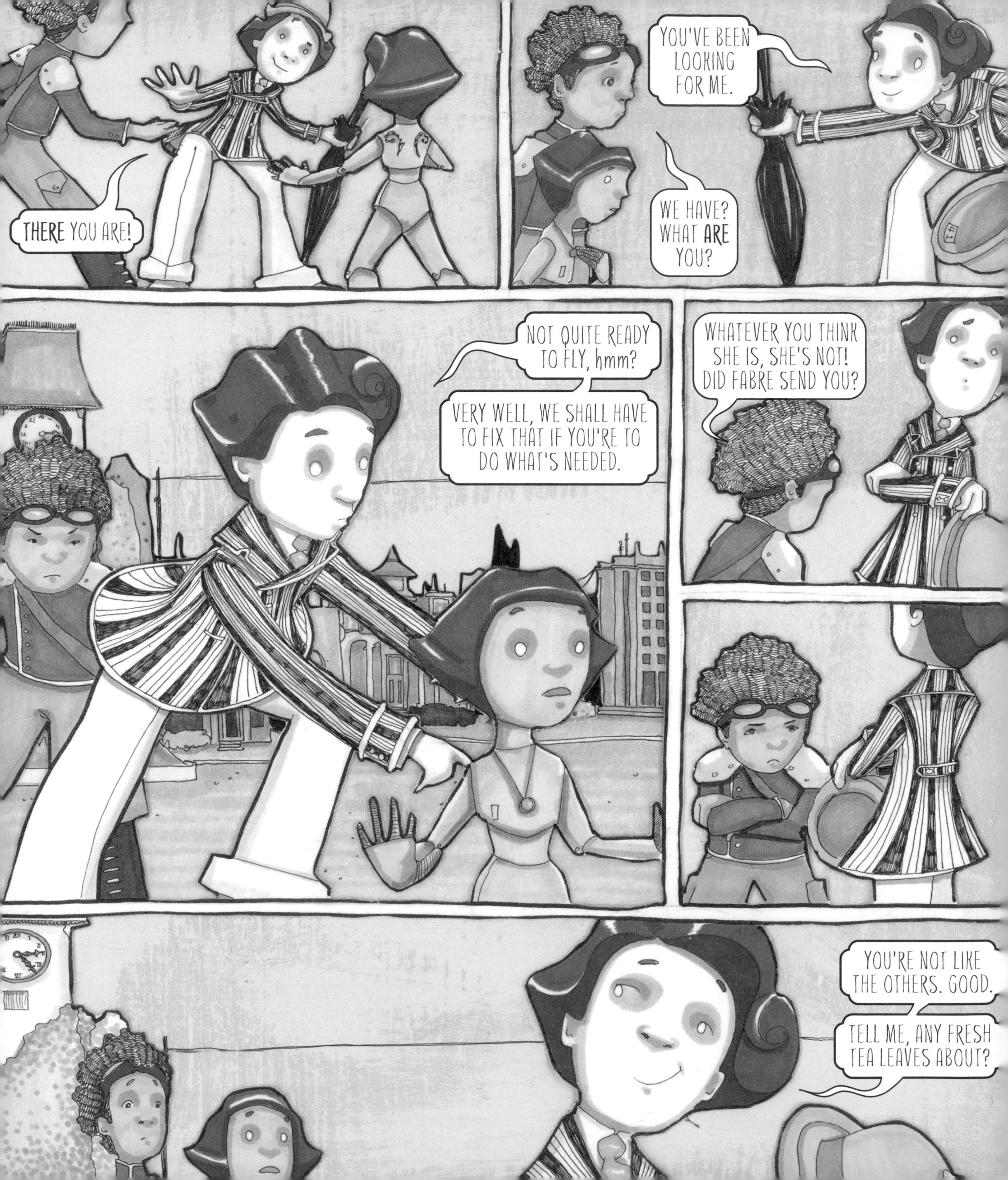
THERE YOU ARE!
YOU'VE BEEN LOOKING FOR ME.
WE HAVE? WHAT ARE YOU?
NOT QUITE READY TO FLY, hmm?
VERY WELL, WE SHALL HAVE TO FIX THAT IF YOU'RE TO DO WHAT'S NEEDED.
WHATEVER YOU THINK SHE IS, SHE'S NOT! DID FABRE SEND YOU?
YOU'RE NOT LIKE THE OTHERS. GOOD.
TELL ME, ANY FRESH TEA LEAVES ABOUT?

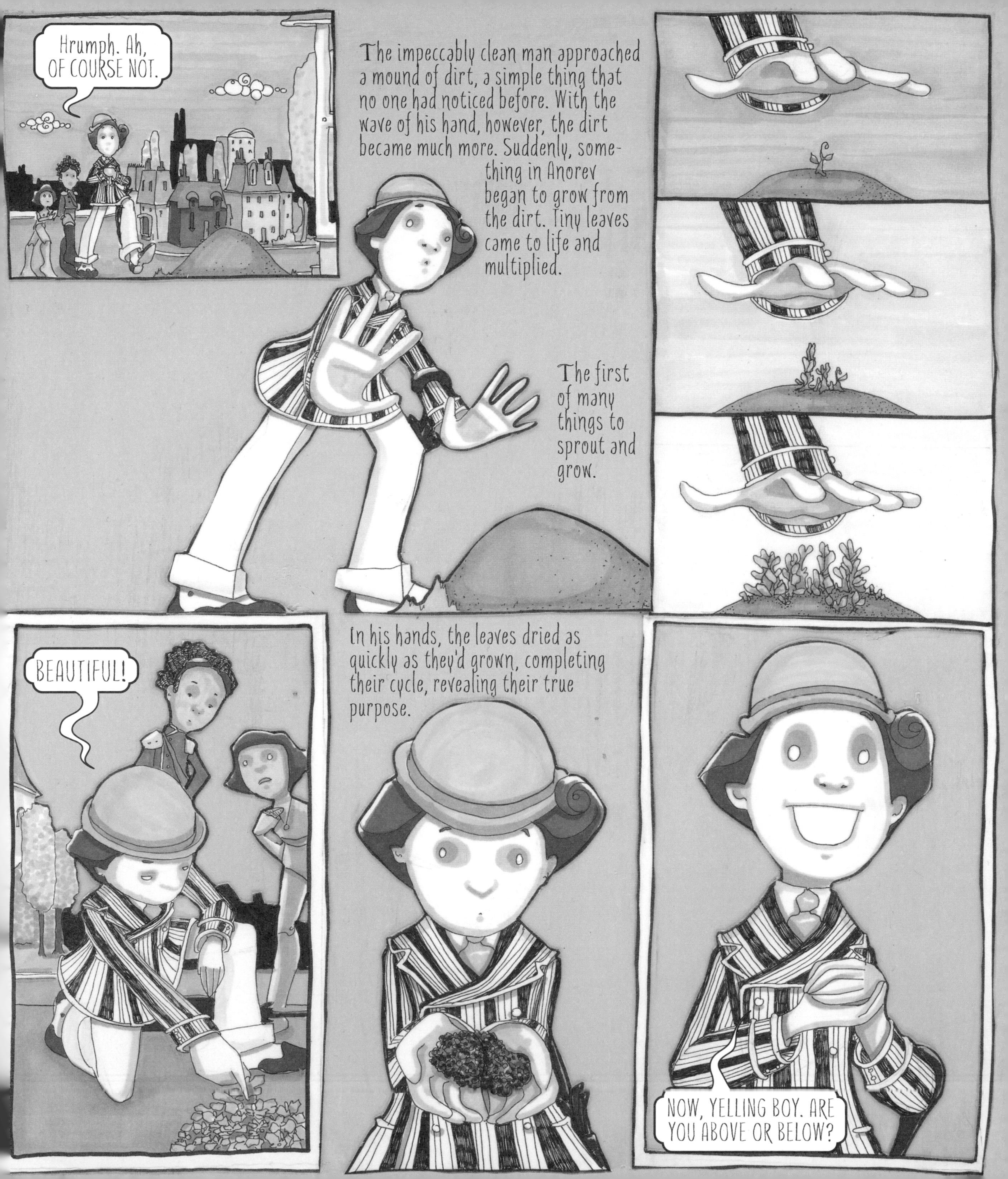
Hrumph. Ah, OF COURSE NOT.
The impeccably clean man approached a mound of dirt, a simple thing that no one had noticed before. With the wave of his hand, however, the dirt became much more. Suddenly, something in Anorev began to grow from the dirt. Tiny leaves came to life and multiplied.
The first of many things to sprout and grow.
BEAUTIFUL!
In his hands, the leaves dried as quickly as they'd grown, completing their cycle, revealing their true purpose.
NOW, YELLING BOY. ARE YOU ABOVE OR BELOW?

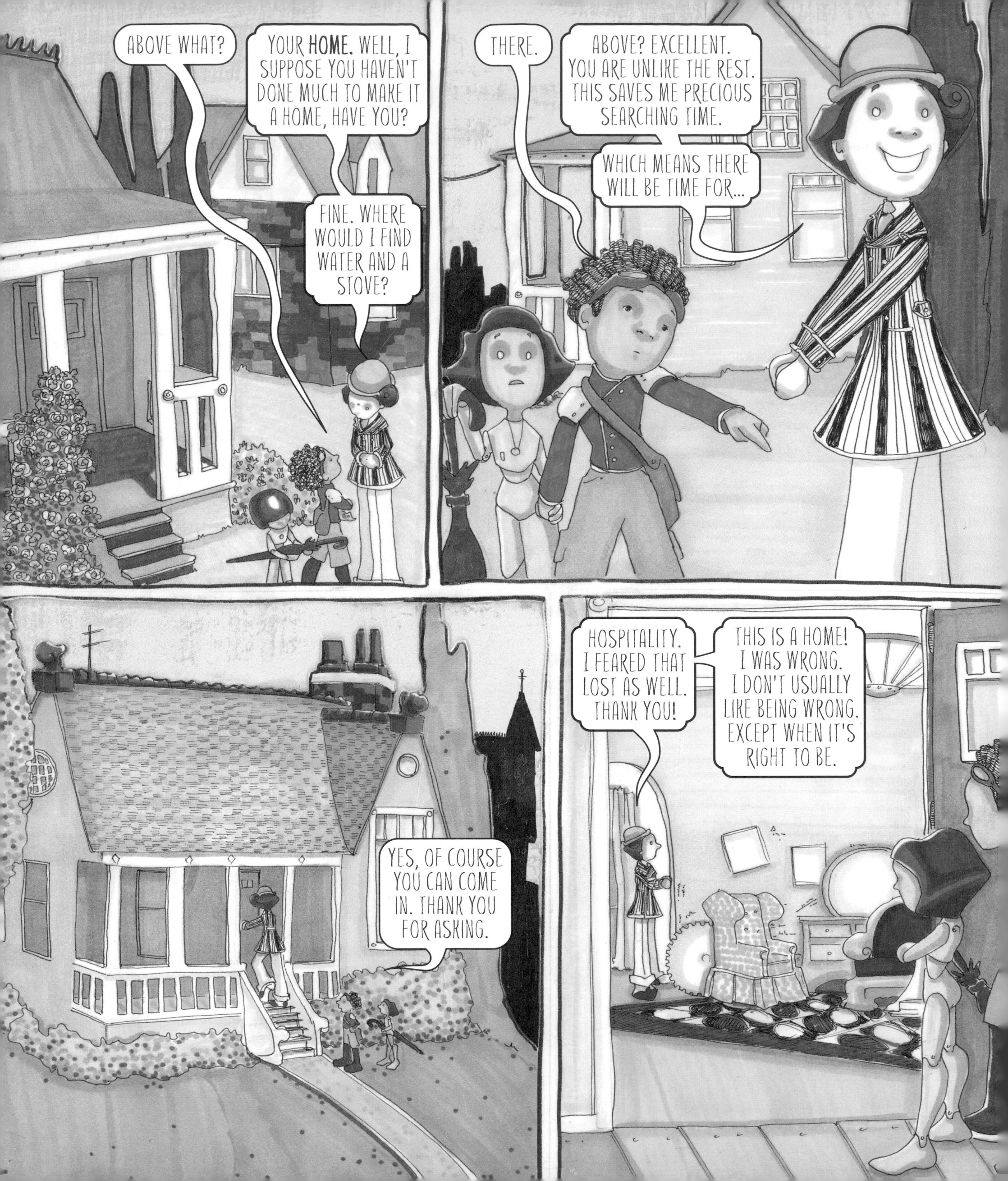
ABOVE WHAT?
YOUR **HOME.** WELL, I SUPPOSE YOU HAVEN'T DONE MUCH TO MAKE IT A HOME, HAVE YOU?
FINE. WHERE WOULD I FIND WATER AND A STOVE?
THERE.
ABOVE? EXCELLENT. YOU ARE UNLIKE THE REST. THIS SAVES ME PRECIOUS SEARCHING TIME.
WHICH MEANS THERE WILL BE TIME FOR...
YES, OF COURSE YOU CAN COME IN. THANK YOU FOR ASKING.
HOSPITALITY. I FEARED THAT LOST AS WELL. THANK YOU!
THIS IS A HOME! I WAS WRONG. I DON'T USUALLY LIKE BEING WRONG. EXCEPT WHEN IT'S RIGHT TO BE.

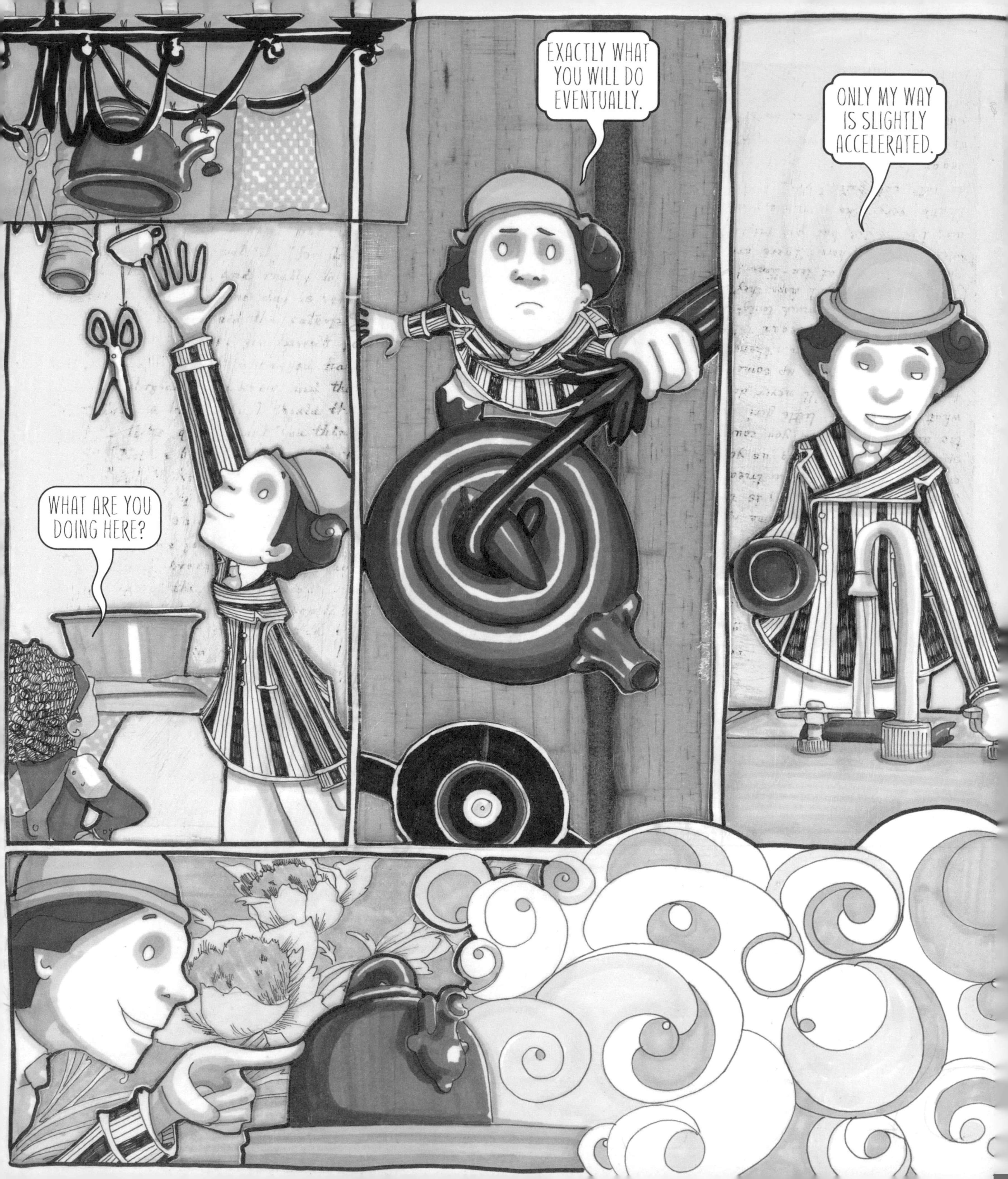
WHAT ARE YOU DOING HERE?
EXACTLY WHAT YOU WILL DO EVENTUALLY.
ONLY MY WAY IS SLIGHTLY ACCELERATED.

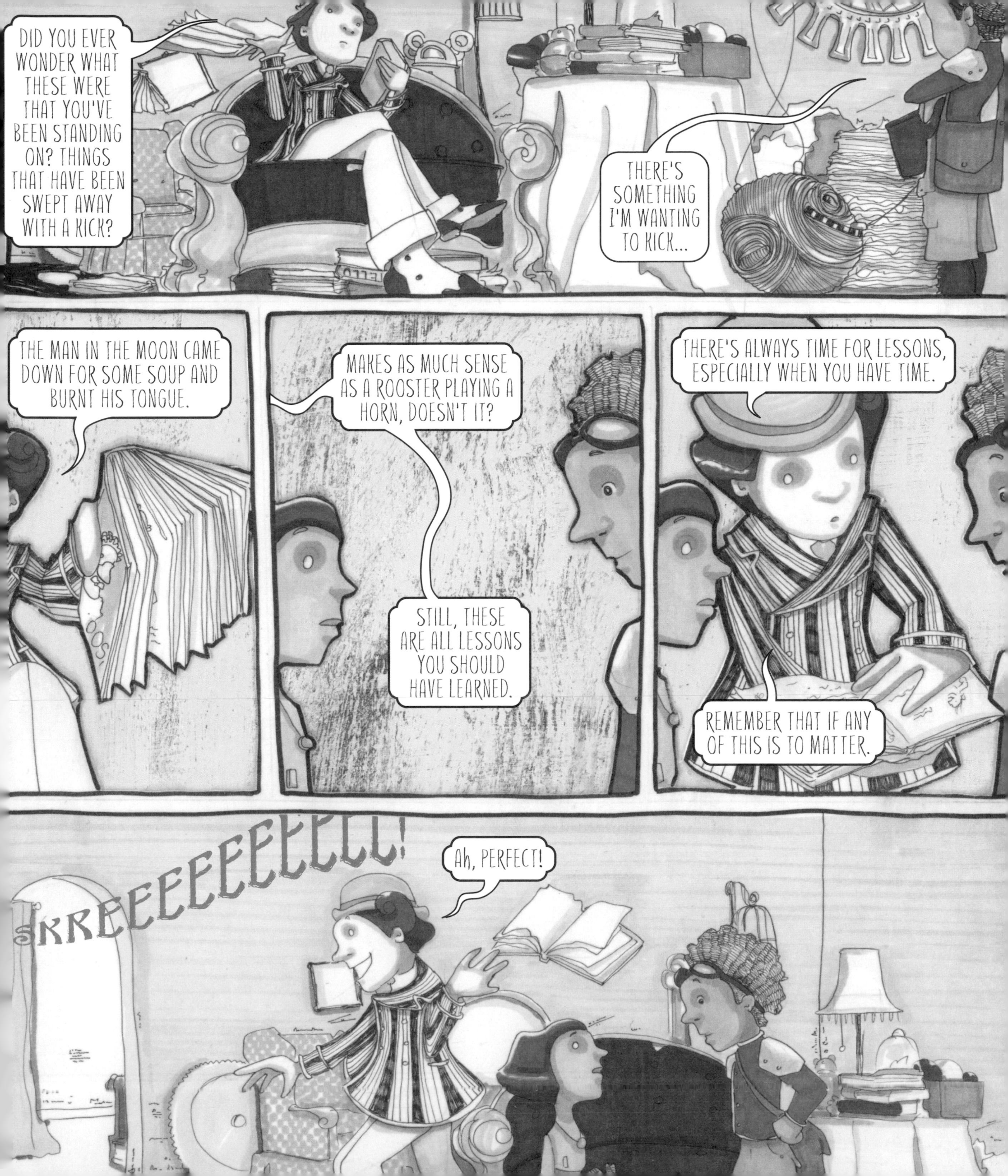
DID YOU EVER WONDER WHAT THESE WERE THAT YOU'VE BEEN STANDING ON? THINGS THAT HAVE BEEN SWEPT AWAY WITH A KICK?
THERE'S SOMETHING I'M WANTING TO KICK...
THE MAN IN THE MOON CAME DOWN FOR SOME SOUP AND BURNT HIS TONGUE.
MAKES AS MUCH SENSE AS A ROOSTER PLAYING A HORN, DOESN'T IT?
STILL, THESE ARE ALL LESSONS YOU SHOULD HAVE LEARNED.
THERE'S ALWAYS TIME FOR LESSONS, ESPECIALLY WHEN YOU HAVE TIME.
REMEMBER THAT IF ANY OF THIS IS TO MATTER.
SKREEEEEEEEELLL!
Ah, PERFECT!

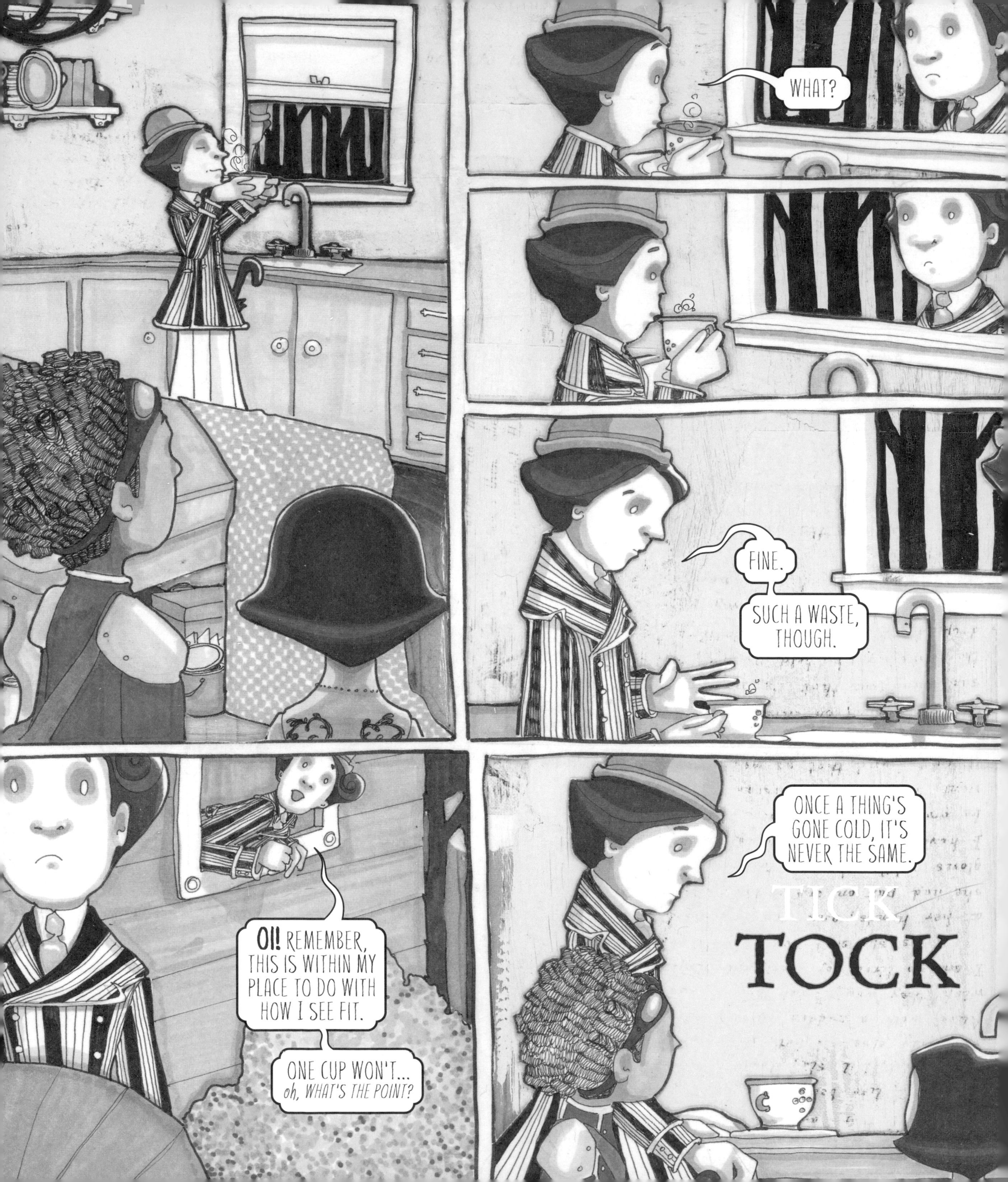
WHAT?
FINE.
SUCH A WASTE, THOUGH.
OI! REMEMBER, THIS IS WITHIN MY PLACE TO DO WITH HOW I SEE FIT.
ONE CUP WON'T... oh, WHAT'S THE POINT?
ONCE A THING'S GONE COLD, IT'S NEVER THE SAME.
TICK
TOCK

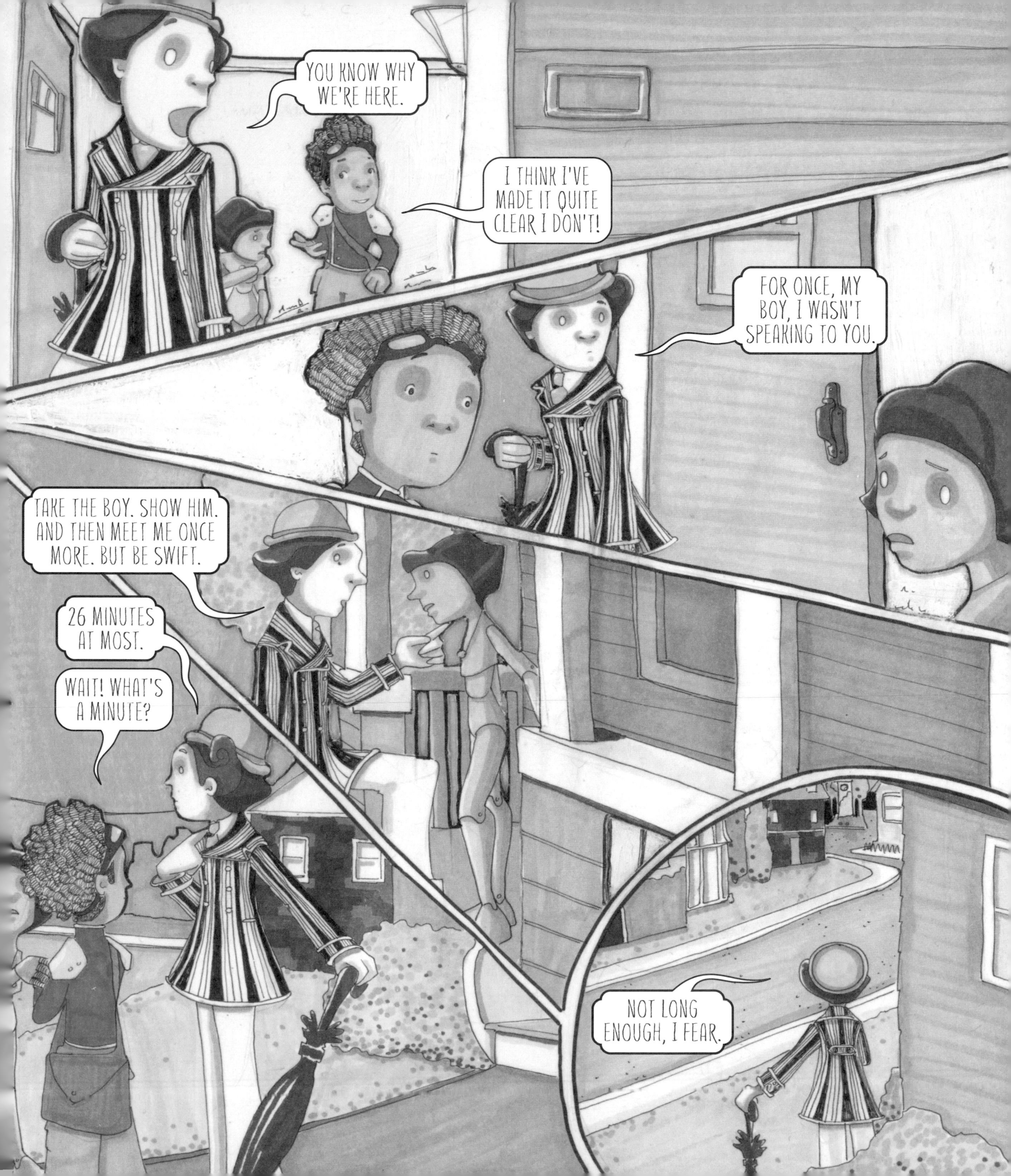
YOU KNOW WHY WE'RE HERE.
I THINK I'VE MADE IT QUITE CLEAR I DON'T!
FOR ONCE, MY BOY, I WASN'T SPEAKING TO YOU.
TAKE THE BOY. SHOW HIM. AND THEN MEET ME ONCE MORE. BUT BE SWIFT.
26 MINUTES AT MOST.
WAIT! WHAT'S A MINUTE?
NOT LONG ENOUGH, I FEAR.

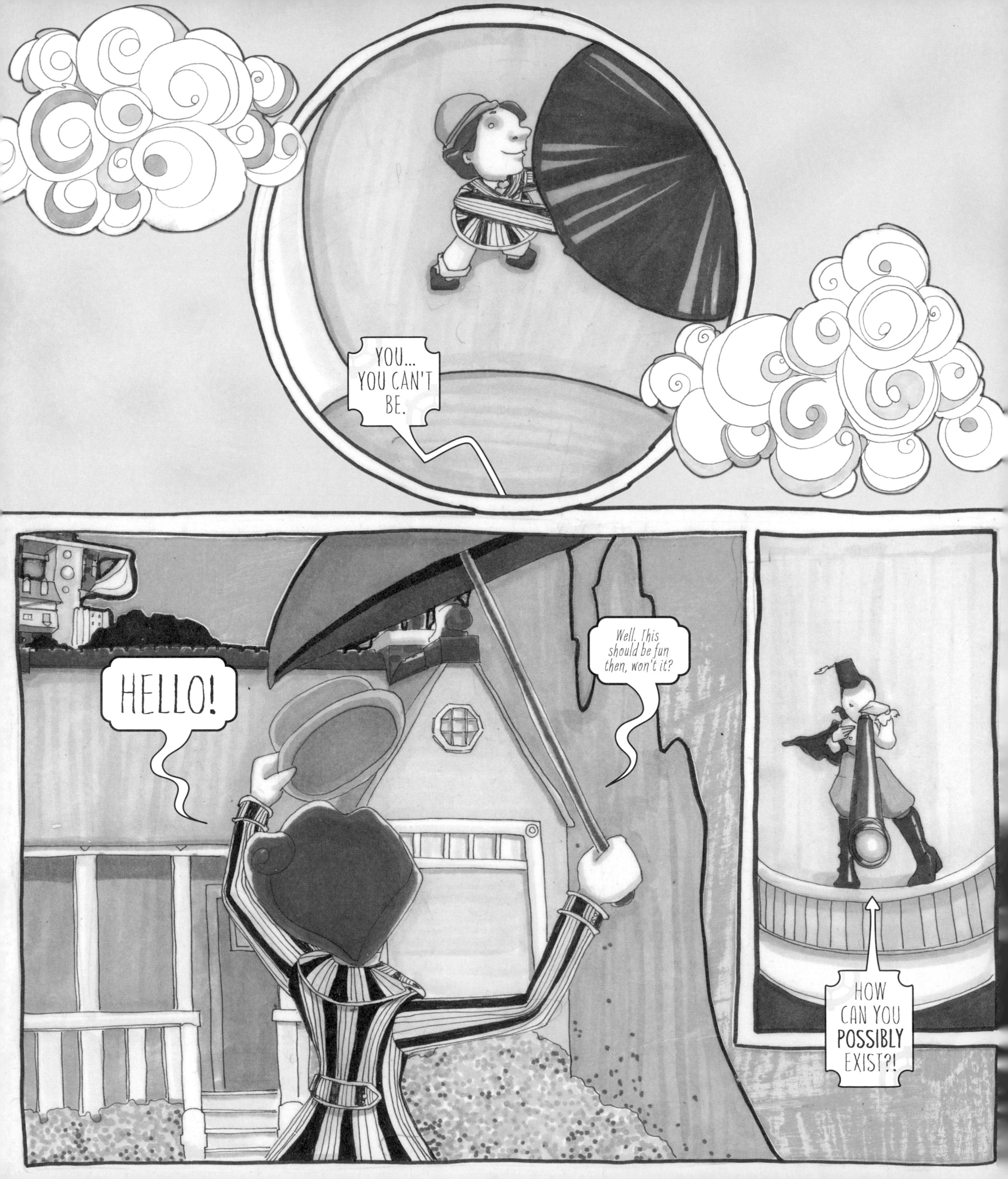
YOU... YOU CAN'T BE.
HELLO!
Well. This should be fun then, won't it?
HOW CAN YOU POSSIBLY EXIST?!

No matter where you went in Anorev, there was one structure you could always see. Some called it a contraption, others a fool's grasp. Three called it "Home."

It was here that gave Fabre the name of "Highness," for that is exactly what he aspired to be.

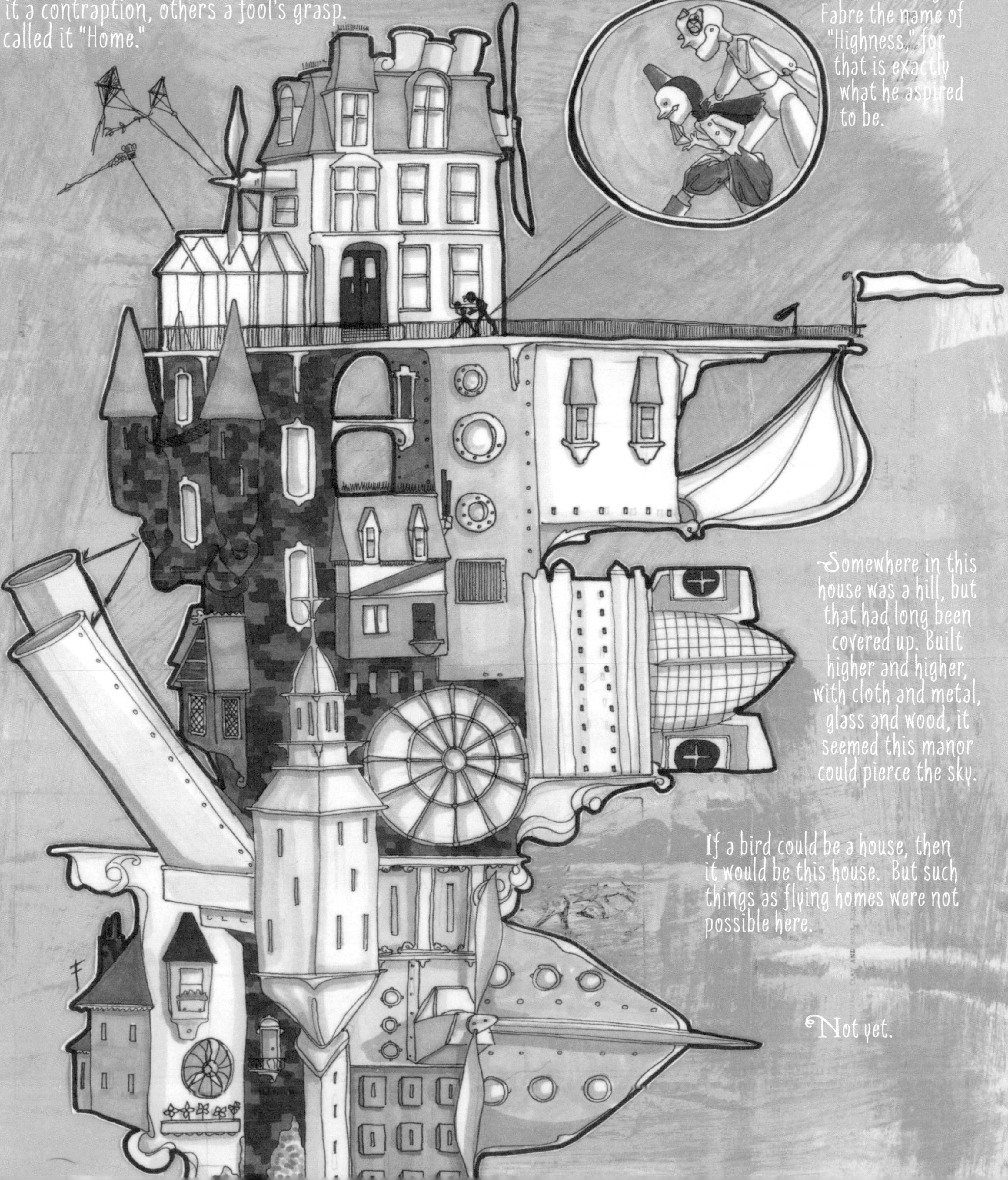

Somewhere in this house was a hill, but that had long been covered up. Built higher and higher, with cloth and metal, glass and wood, it seemed this manor could pierce the sky.

If a bird could be a house, then it would be this house. But such things as flying homes were not possible here.

Not yet.

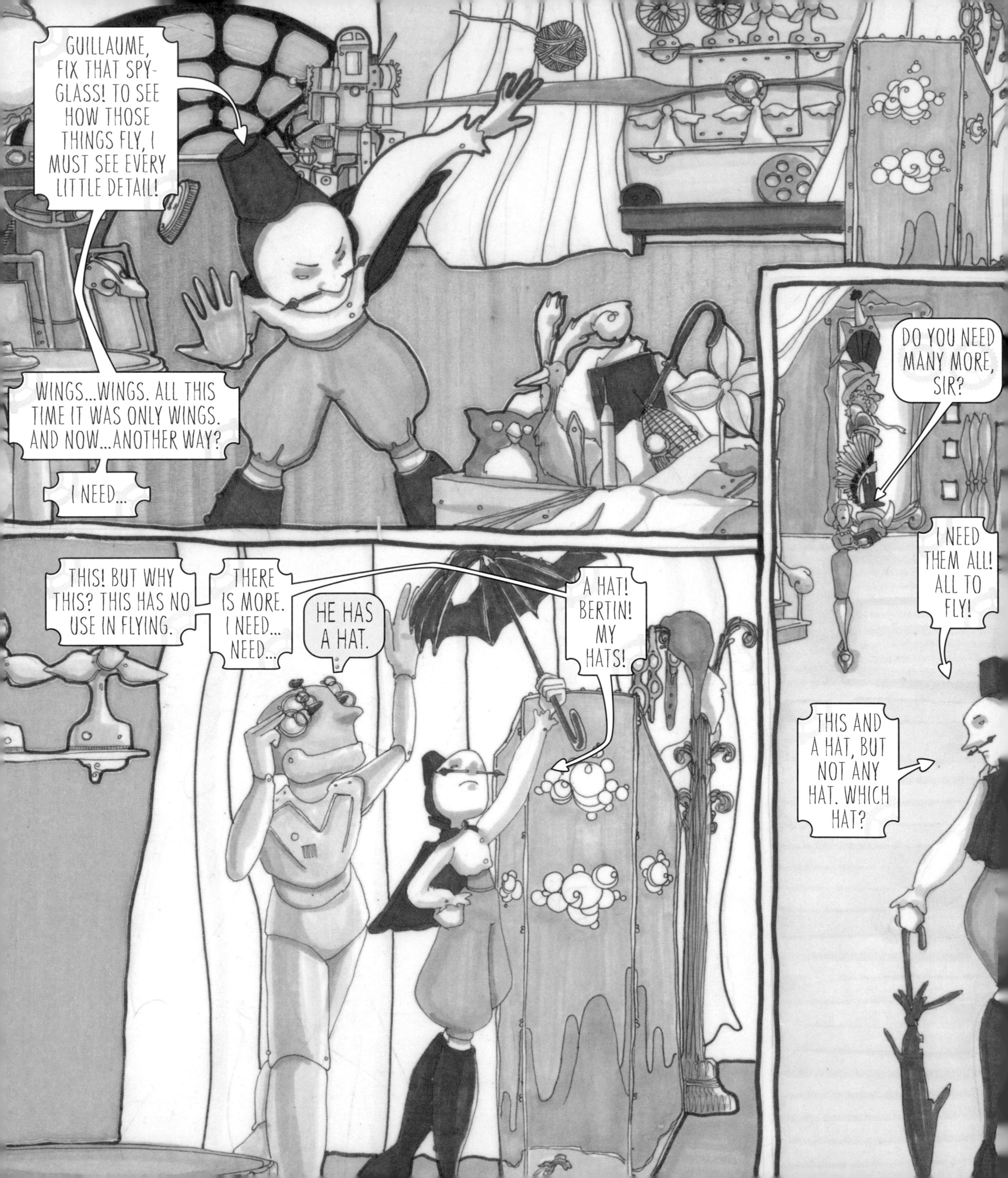
GUILLAUME, FIX THAT SPY-GLASS! TO SEE HOW THOSE THINGS FLY, I MUST SEE EVERY LITTLE DETAIL!
WINGS...WINGS. ALL THIS TIME IT WAS ONLY WINGS. AND NOW...ANOTHER WAY?
I NEED...
DO YOU NEED MANY MORE, SIR?
I NEED THEM ALL! ALL TO FLY!
THIS! BUT WHY THIS? THIS HAS NO USE IN FLYING.
THERE IS MORE. I NEED... NEED...
HE HAS A HAT.
A HAT! BERTIN! MY HATS!
THIS AND A HAT, BUT NOT ANY HAT. WHICH HAT?

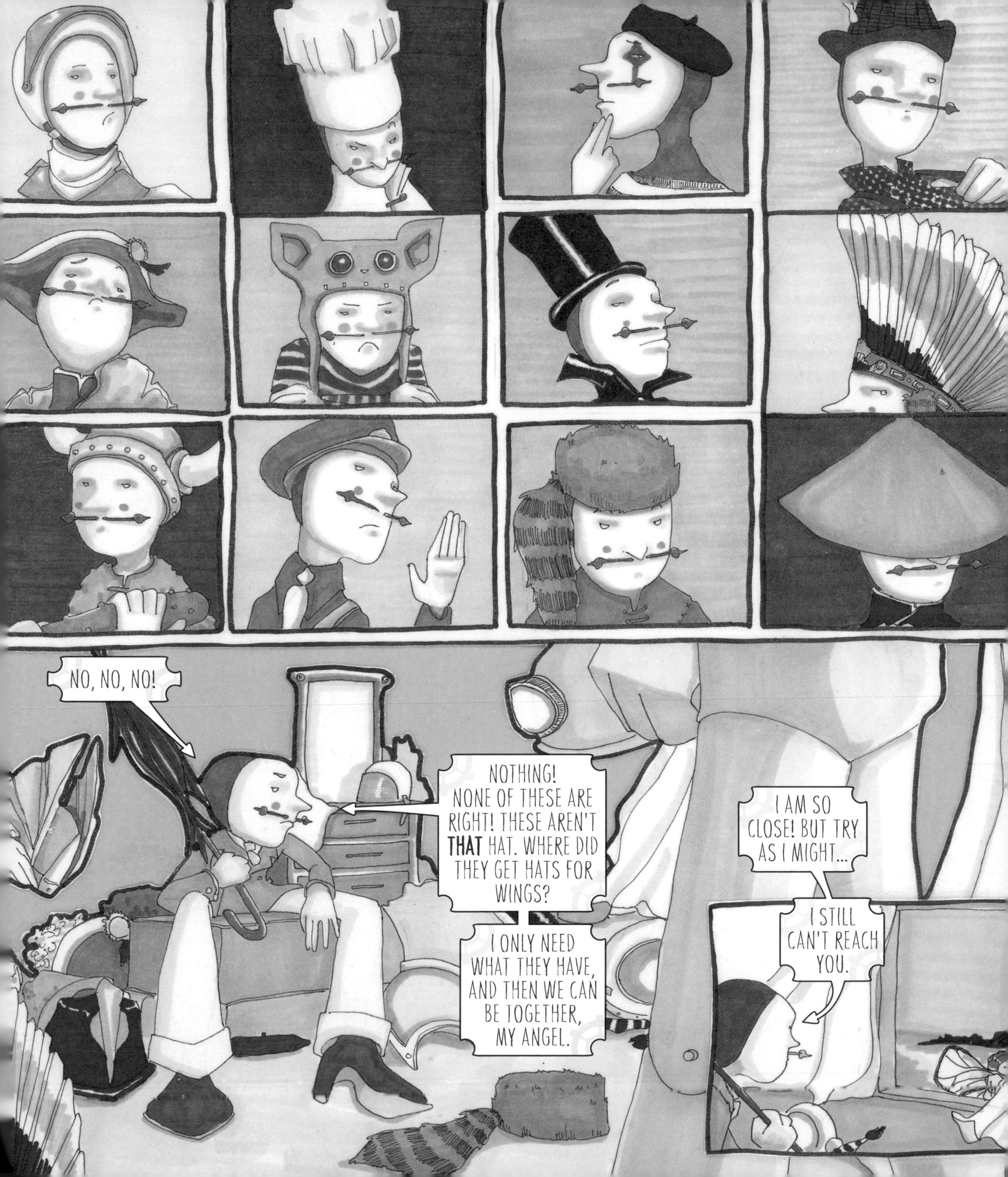
NO, NO, NO!
NOTHING! NONE OF THESE ARE RIGHT! THESE AREN'T **THAT** HAT. WHERE DID THEY GET HATS FOR WINGS?
I ONLY NEED WHAT THEY HAVE, AND THEN WE CAN BE TOGETHER, MY ANGEL.
I AM SO CLOSE! BUT TRY AS I MIGHT...
I STILL CAN'T REACH YOU.

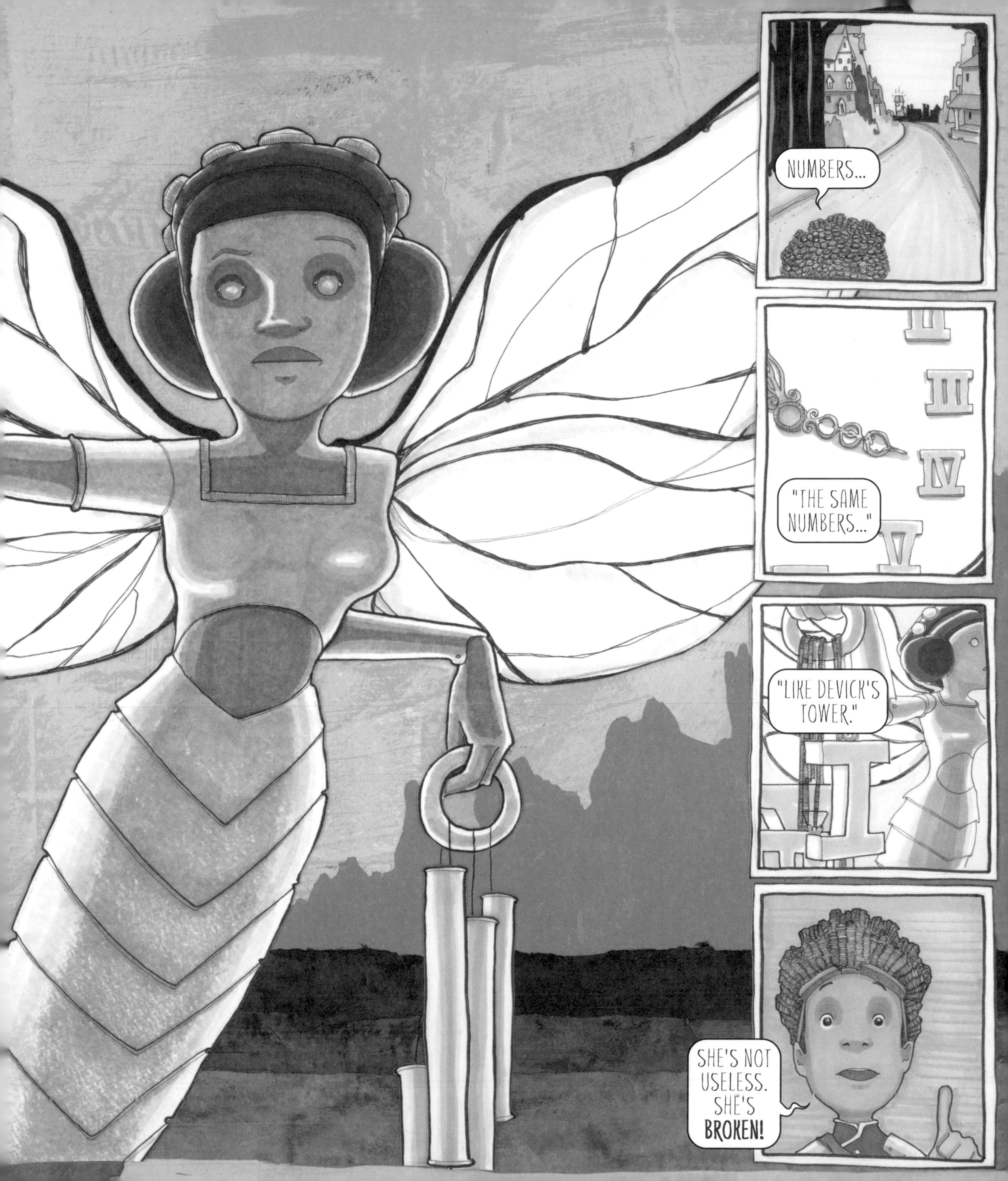
NUMBERS...
"THE SAME NUMBERS..."
"LIKE DEVICK'S TOWER."
SHE'S NOT USELESS. SHE'S **BROKEN!**

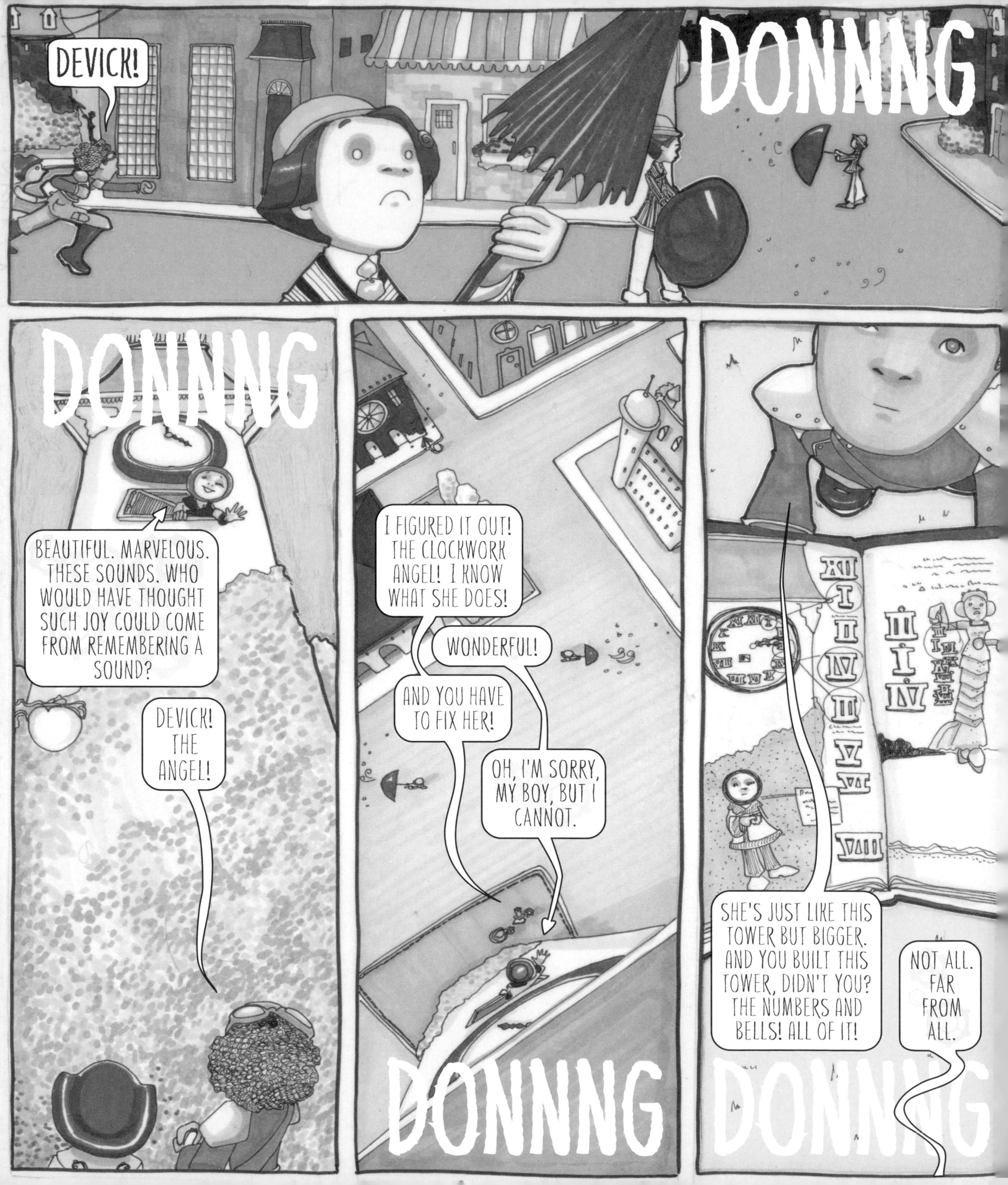
DEVICK!
DONNNG
DONNNG
BEAUTIFUL. MARVELOUS. THESE SOUNDS. WHO WOULD HAVE THOUGHT SUCH JOY COULD COME FROM REMEMBERING A SOUND?
DEVICK! THE ANGEL!
I FIGURED IT OUT! THE CLOCKWORK ANGEL! I KNOW WHAT SHE DOES!
WONDERFUL!
AND YOU HAVE TO FIX HER!
OH, I'M SORRY, MY BOY, BUT I CANNOT.
DONNNG
SHE'S JUST LIKE THIS TOWER BUT BIGGER. AND YOU BUILT THIS TOWER, DIDN'T YOU? THE NUMBERS AND BELLS! ALL OF IT!
NOT ALL. FAR FROM ALL.
DONNNG

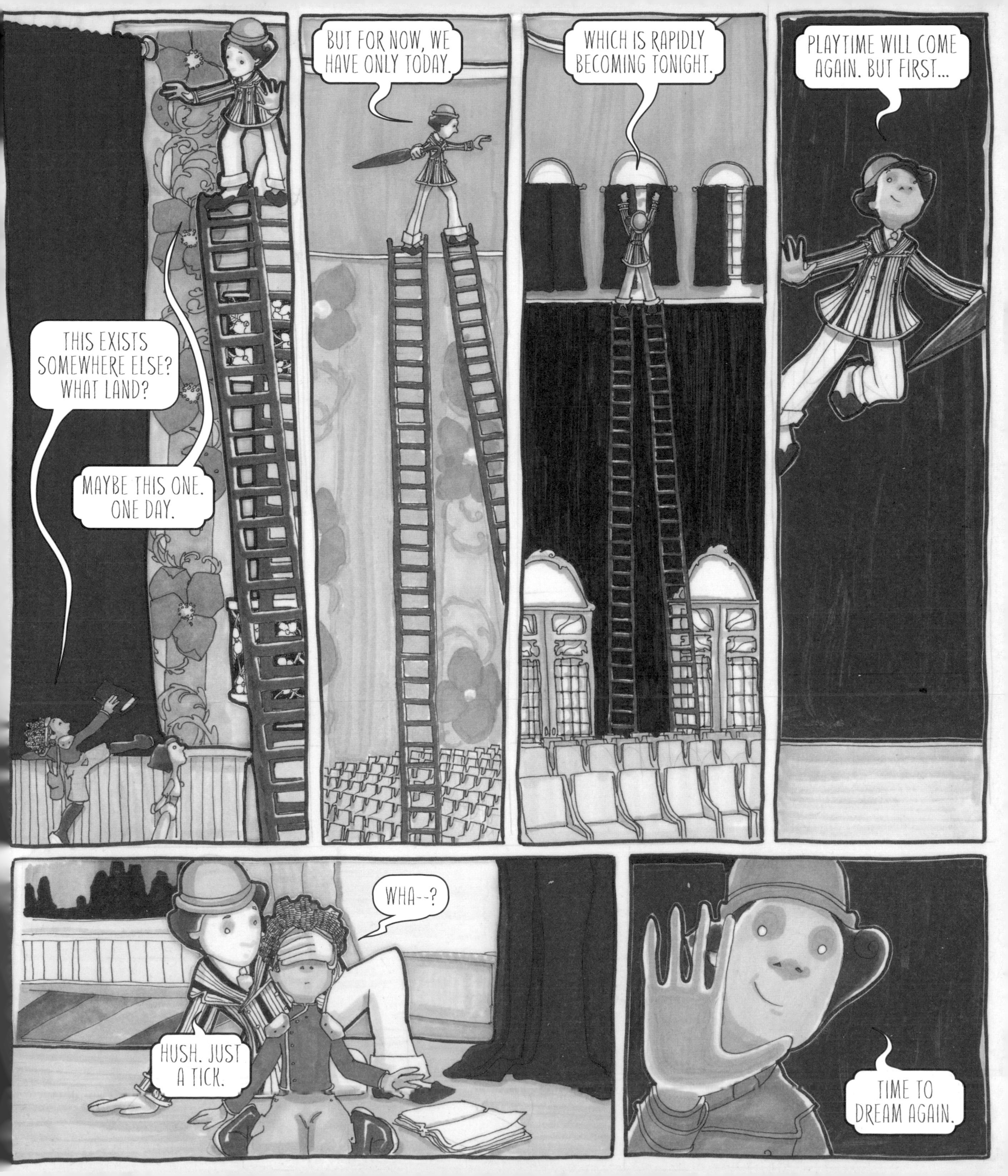
THIS EXISTS SOMEWHERE ELSE? WHAT LAND?
MAYBE THIS ONE. ONE DAY.
BUT FOR NOW, WE HAVE ONLY TODAY.
WHICH IS RAPIDLY BECOMING TONIGHT.
PLAYTIME WILL COME AGAIN. BUT FIRST...
WHA--?
HUSH. JUST A TICK.
TIME TO DREAM AGAIN.

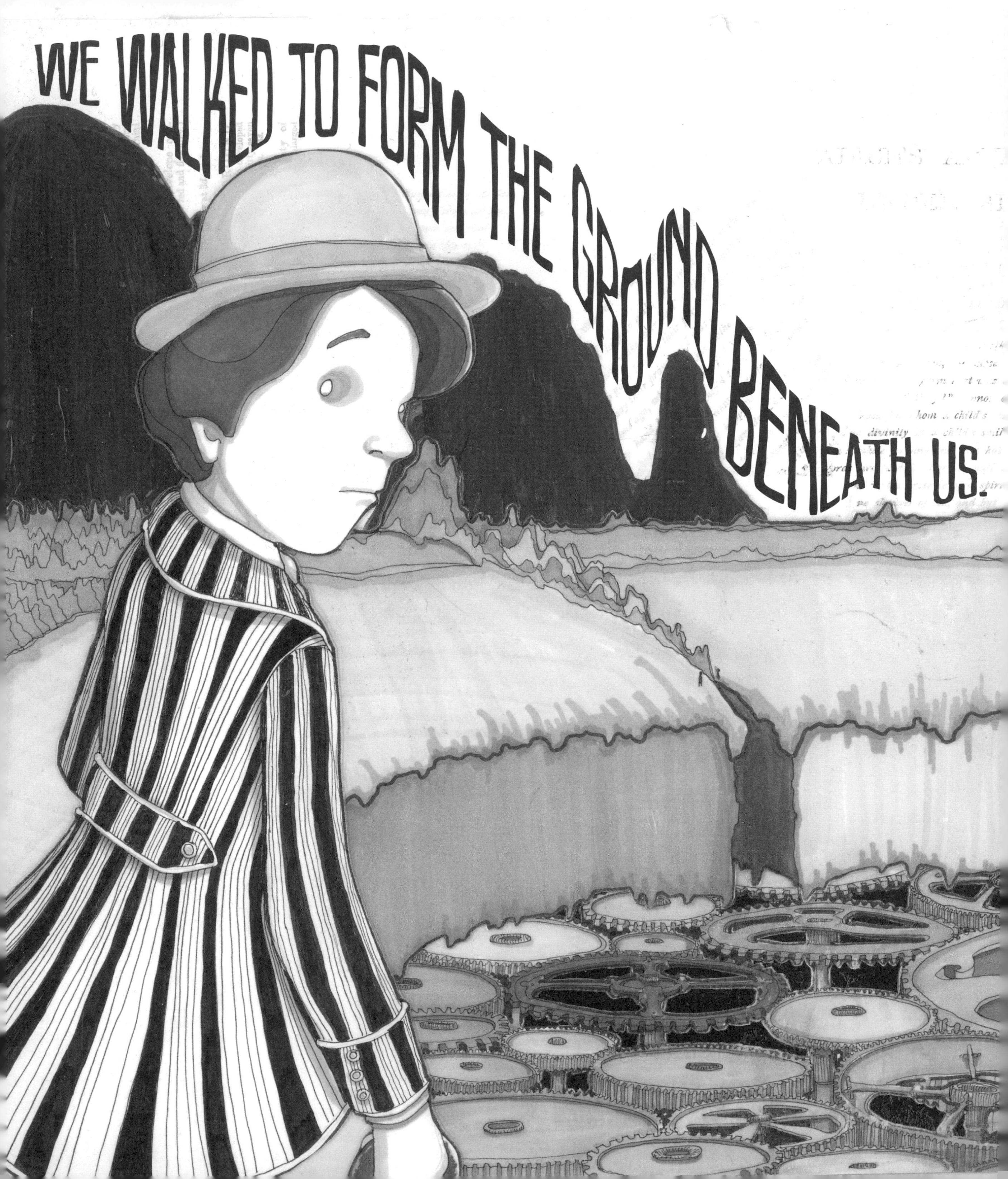
WE WALKED TO FORM THE GROUND BENEATH US.

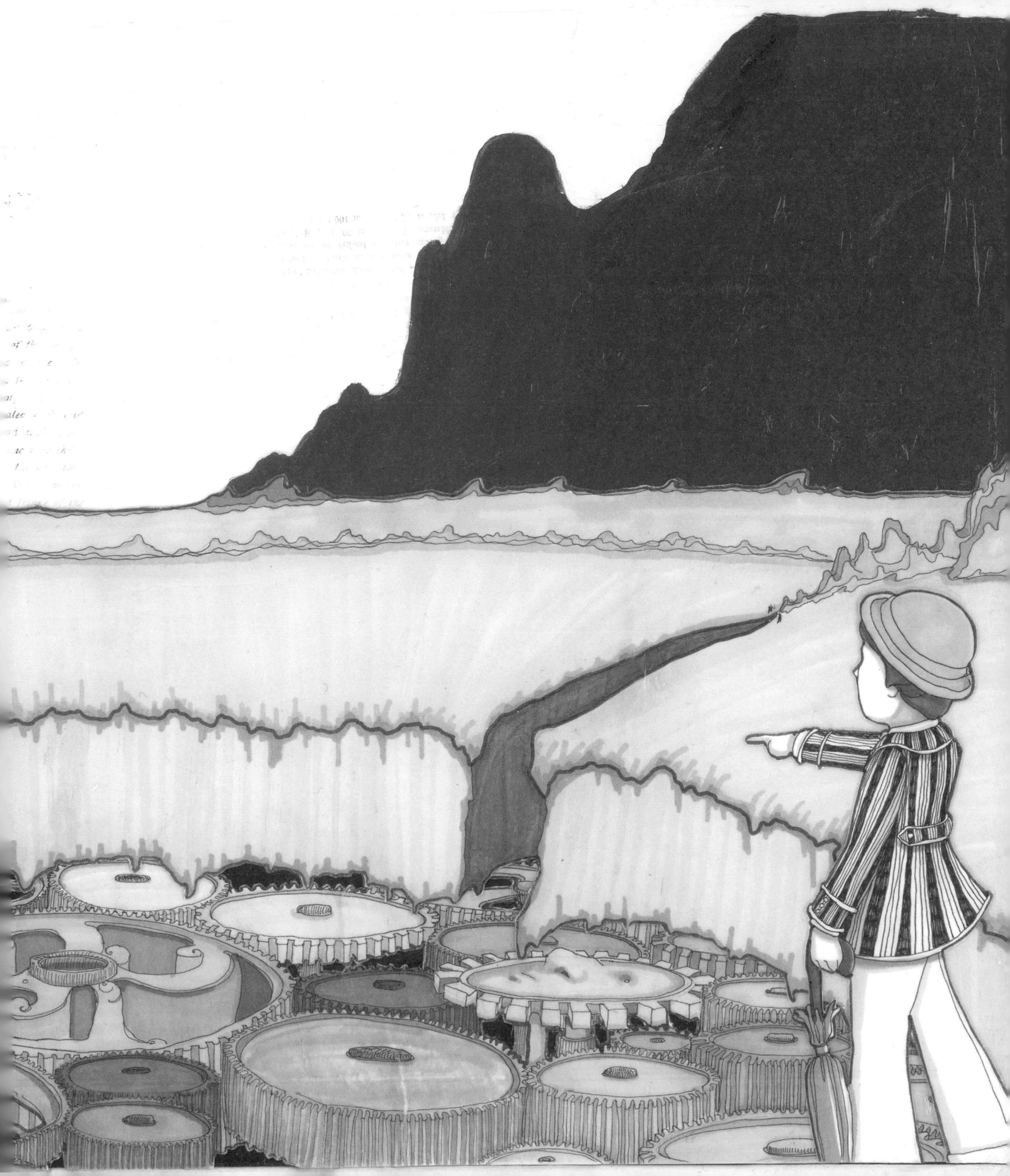

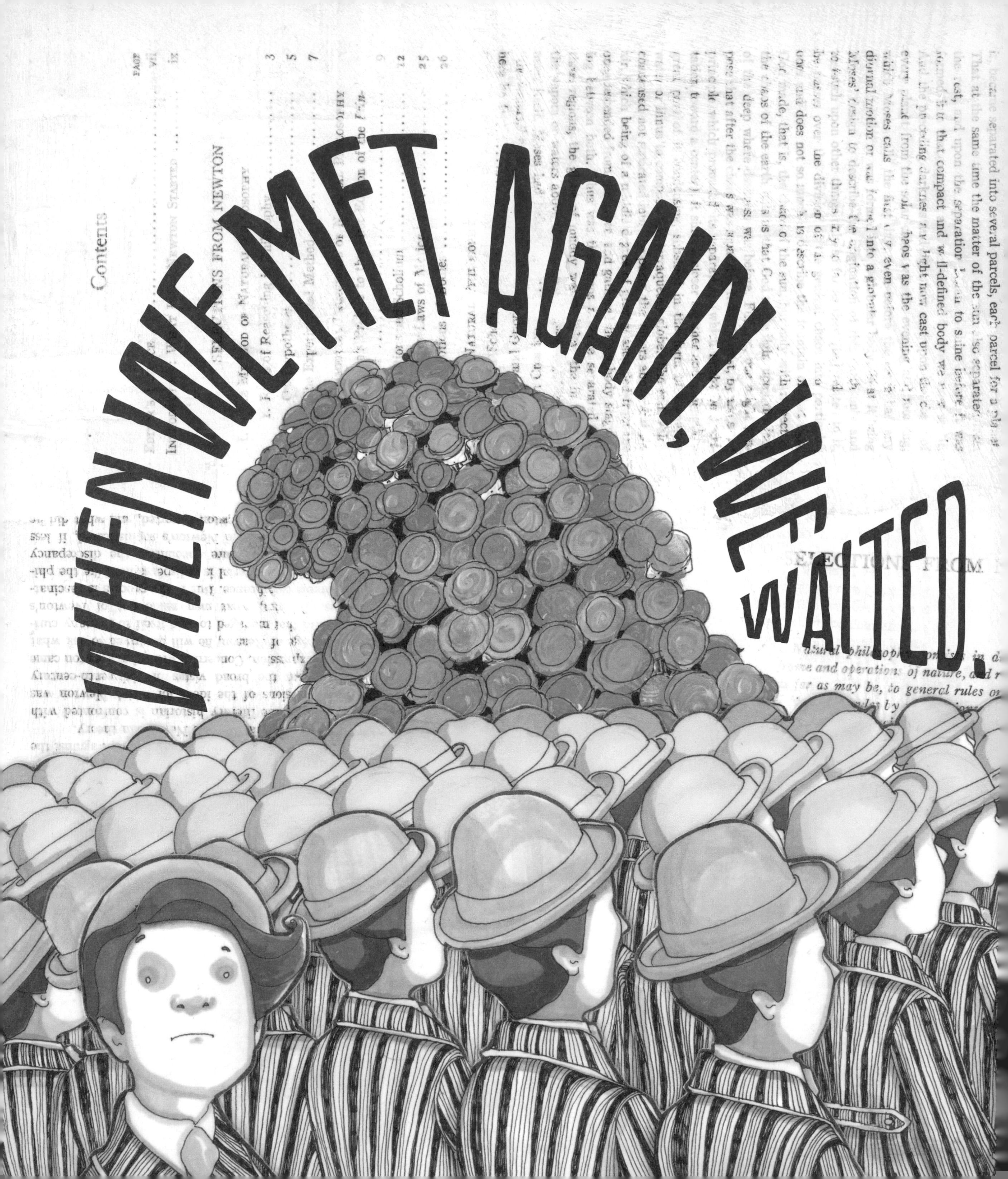
WHEN WE MET AGAIN, WE WAITED.

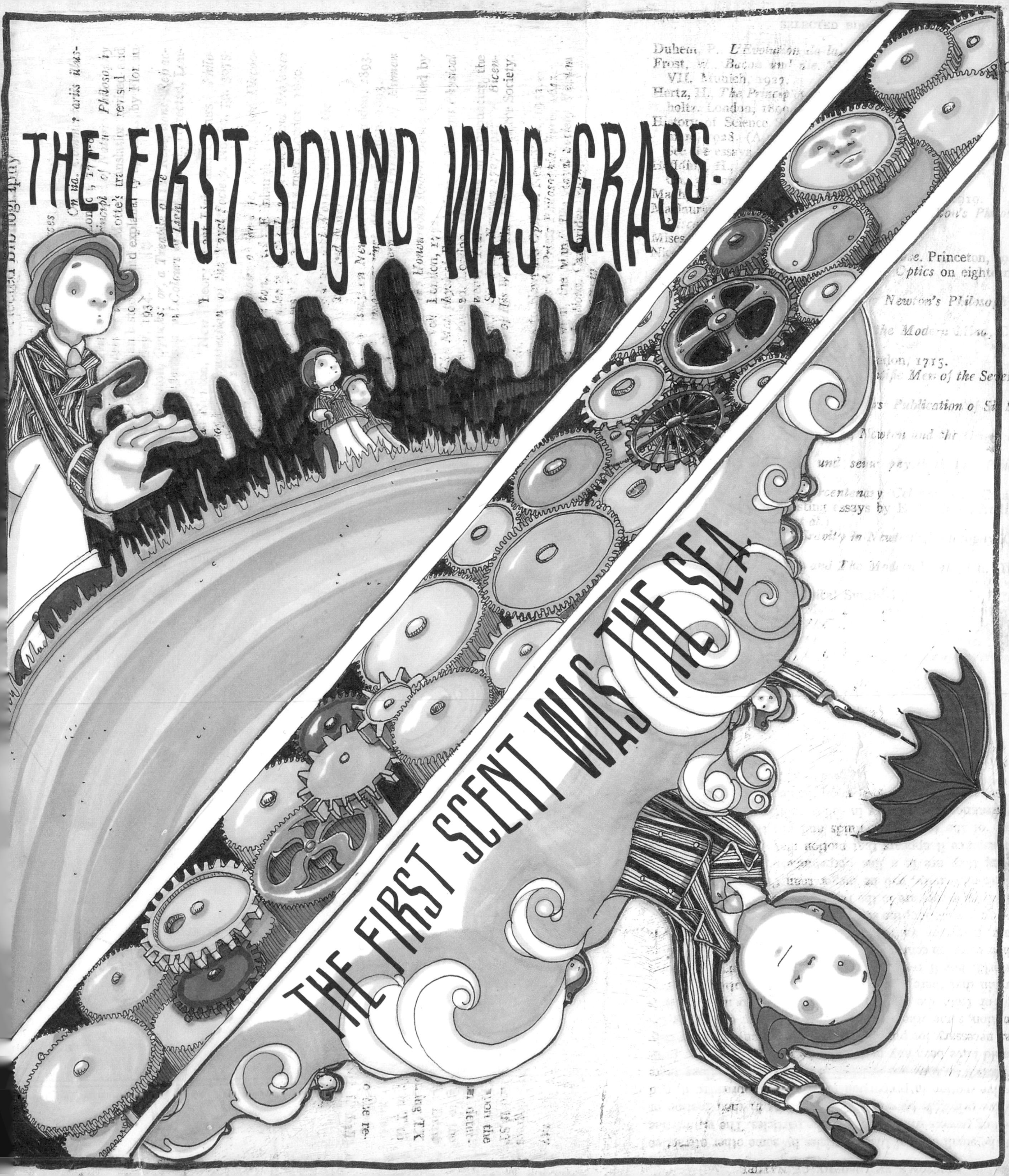
THE FIRST SOUND WAS GRASS.
THE FIRST SCENT WAS THE SEA

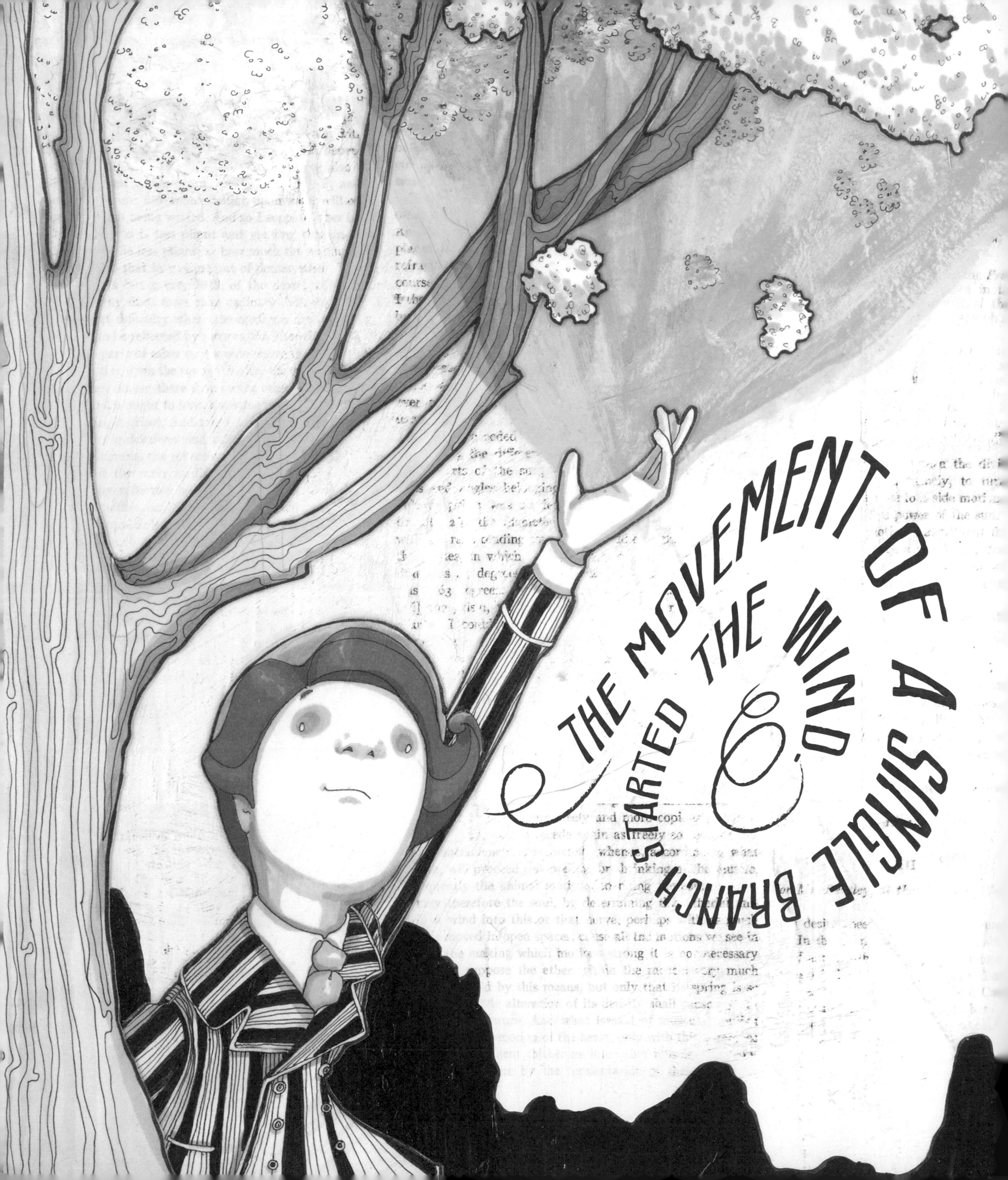
THE MOVEMENT OF A SINGLE BRANCH STARTED THE WIND.

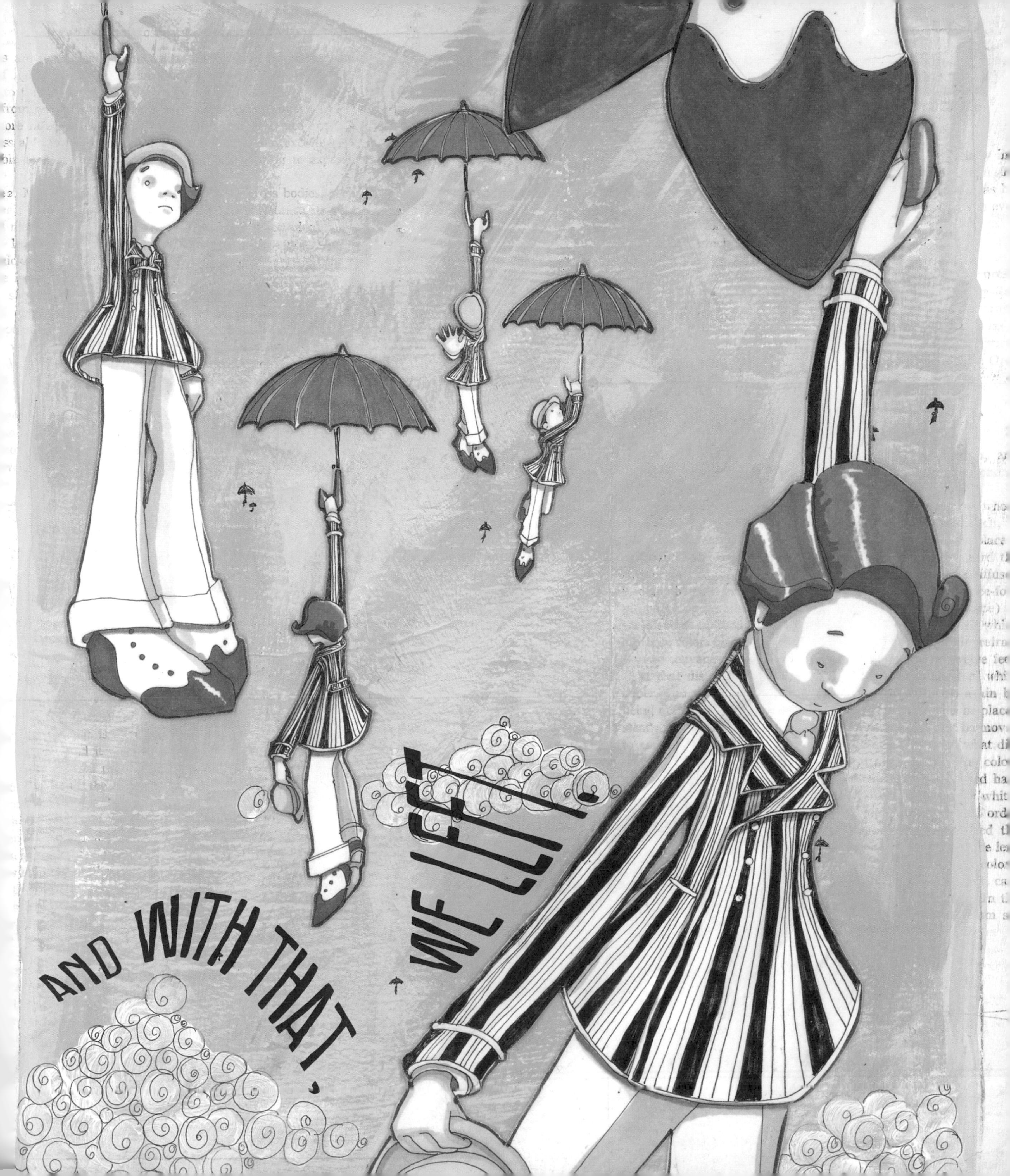
AND WITH THAT, WE LIFT.

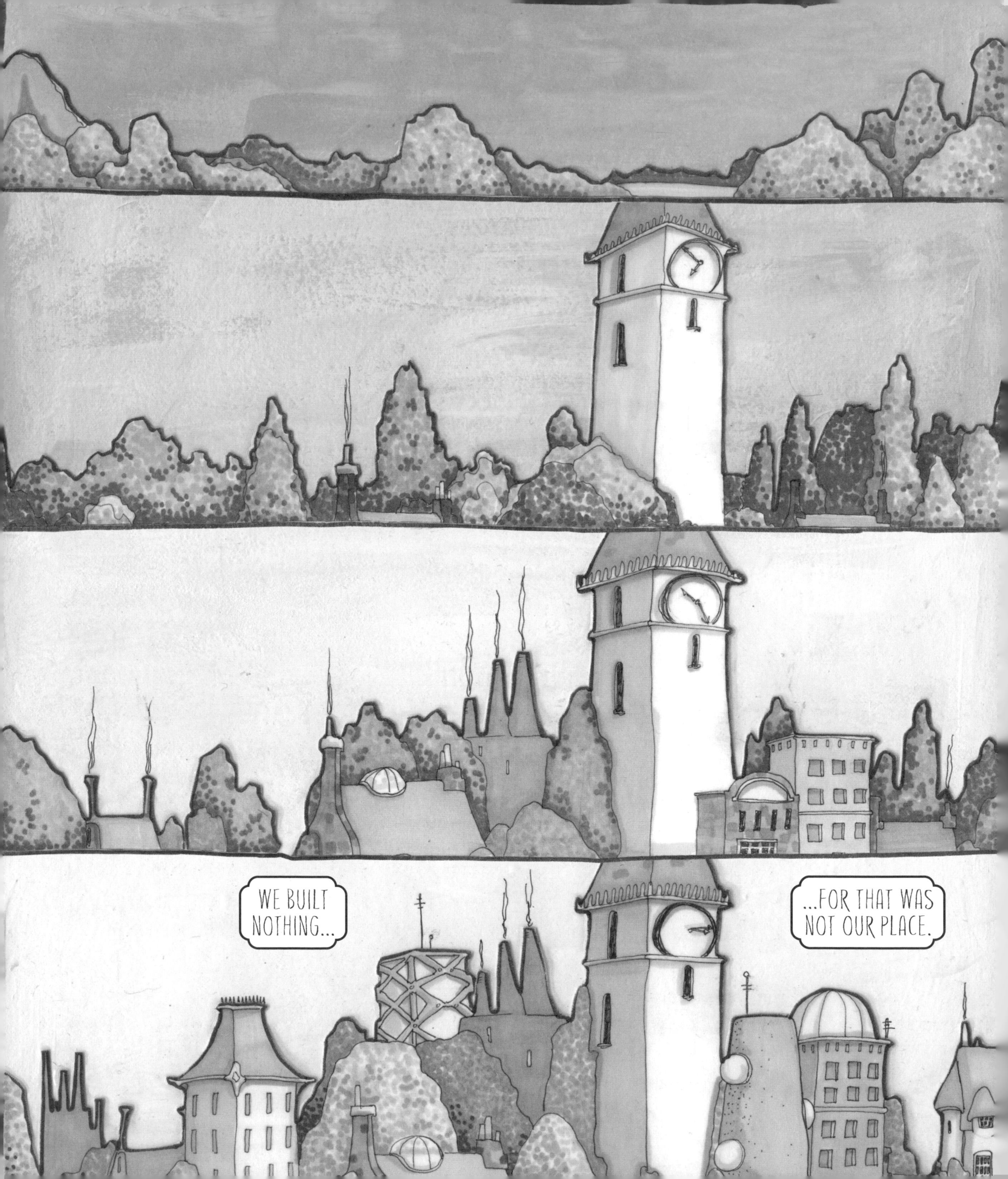
WE BUILT NOTHING...
...FOR THAT WAS NOT OUR PLACE.

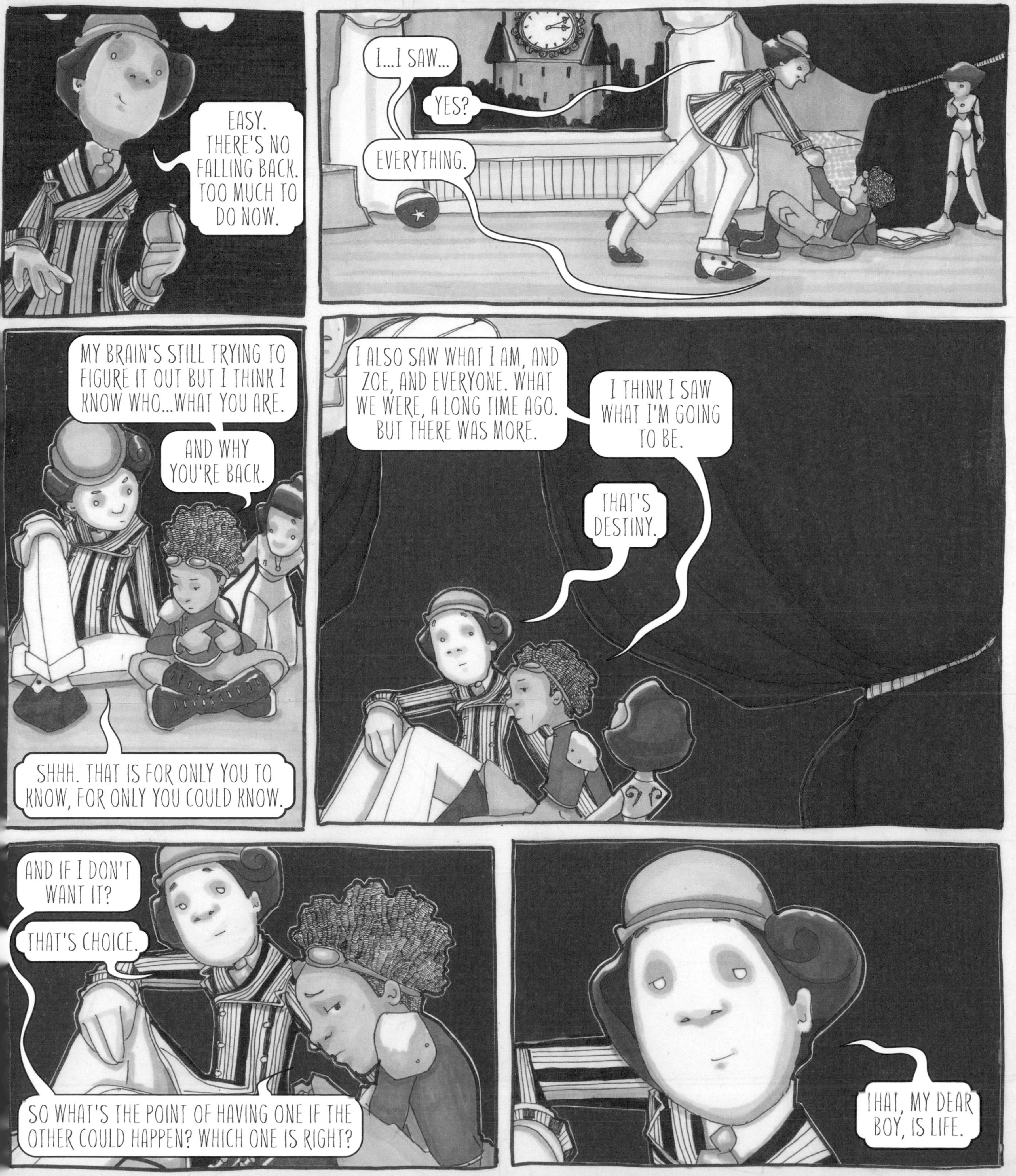
EASY. THERE'S NO FALLING BACK. TOO MUCH TO DO NOW.
I...I SAW...
YES?
EVERYTHING.
MY BRAIN'S STILL TRYING TO FIGURE IT OUT BUT I THINK I KNOW WHO...WHAT YOU ARE.
AND WHY YOU'RE BACK.
SHHH. THAT IS FOR ONLY YOU TO KNOW, FOR ONLY YOU COULD KNOW.
I ALSO SAW WHAT I AM, AND ZOE, AND EVERYONE. WHAT WE WERE, A LONG TIME AGO. BUT THERE WAS MORE.
I THINK I SAW WHAT I'M GOING TO BE.
THAT'S DESTINY.
AND IF I DON'T WANT IT?
THAT'S CHOICE.
SO WHAT'S THE POINT OF HAVING ONE IF THE OTHER COULD HAPPEN? WHICH ONE IS RIGHT?
THAT, MY DEAR BOY, IS LIFE.

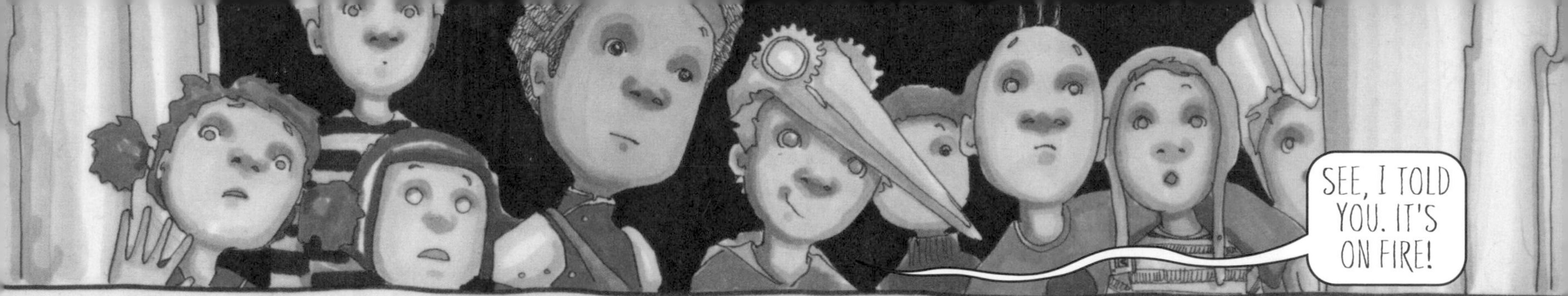
SEE, I TOLD YOU. IT'S ON FIRE!

As everyone and everything rushed out to sungaze, they witnessed the biggest and most significant change of all. As these things do, the day was coming to an end. The longest day that had ever been.

The sun's descent towards the bay left in its wake a myriad of colors that eyes had forgotten they could see, rippling across the sky.

The machines felt a strange sense of relief, as though they knew the time for working was coming to an end, at least for a little while. The children, however, greeted this sight with a different emotion.

They couldn't quite put their finger on why exactly, but it terrified them.

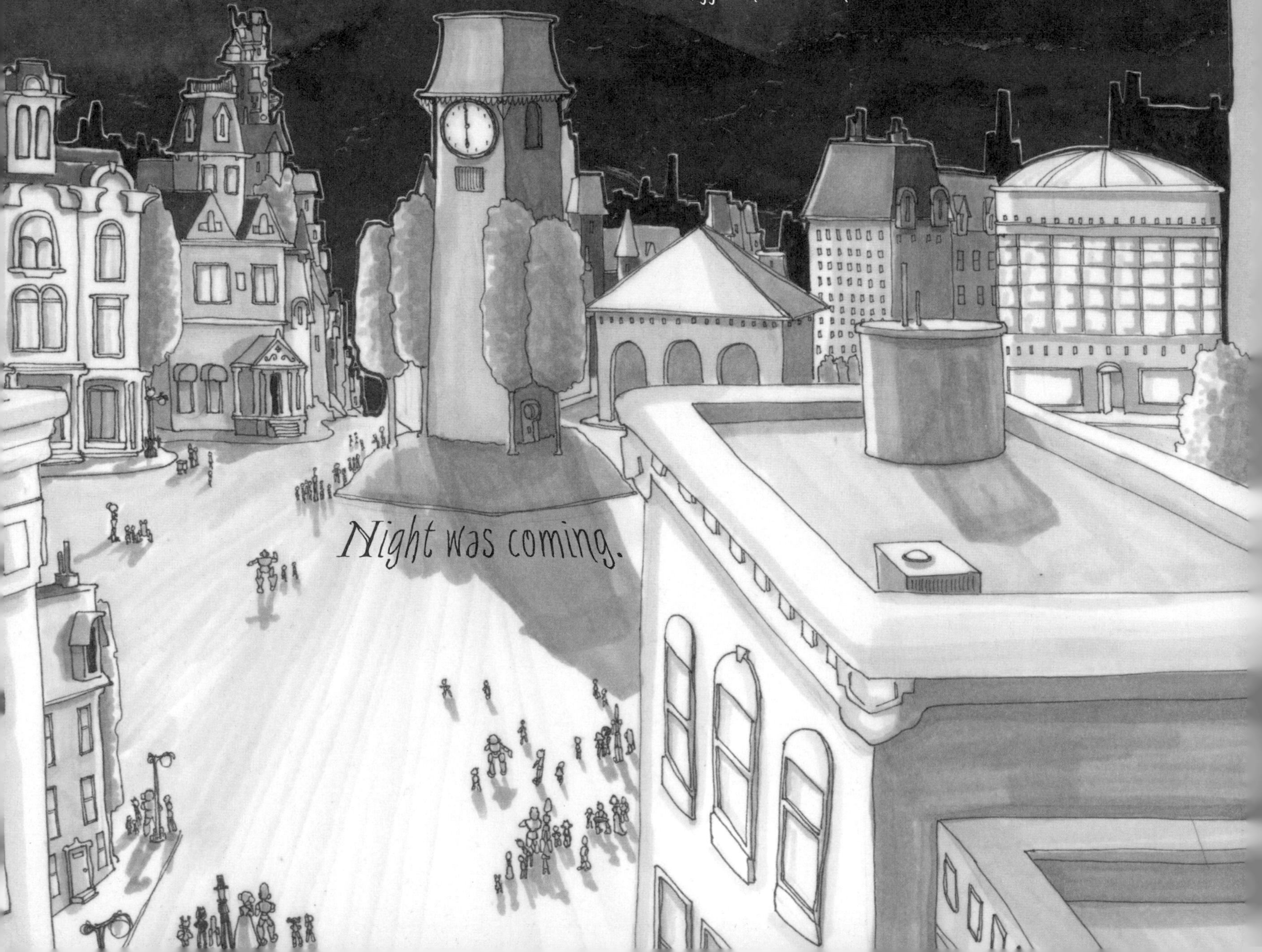

Night was coming.

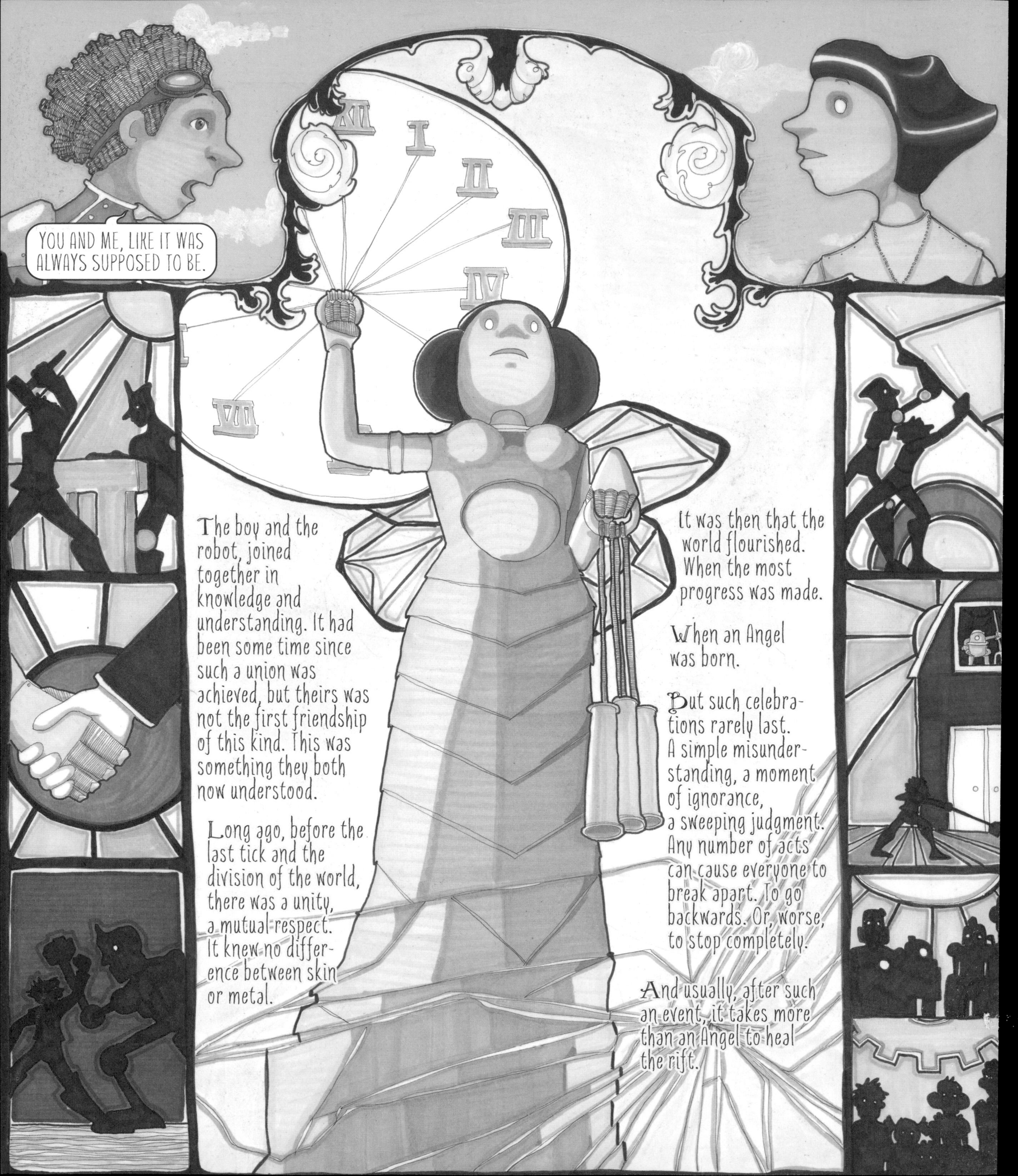
YOU AND ME, LIKE IT WAS ALWAYS SUPPOSED TO BE.
The boy and the robot, joined together in knowledge and understanding. It had been some time since such a union was achieved, but theirs was not the first friendship of this kind. This was something they both now understood.
Long ago, before the last tick and the division of the world, there was a unity, a mutual respect. It knew no difference between skin or metal.
It was then that the world flourished. When the most progress was made.
When an Angel was born.
But such celebrations rarely last. A simple misunderstanding, a moment of ignorance, a sweeping judgment. Any number of acts can cause everyone to break apart. To go backwards. Or, worse, to stop completely.
And usually, after such an event, it takes more than an Angel to heal the rift.

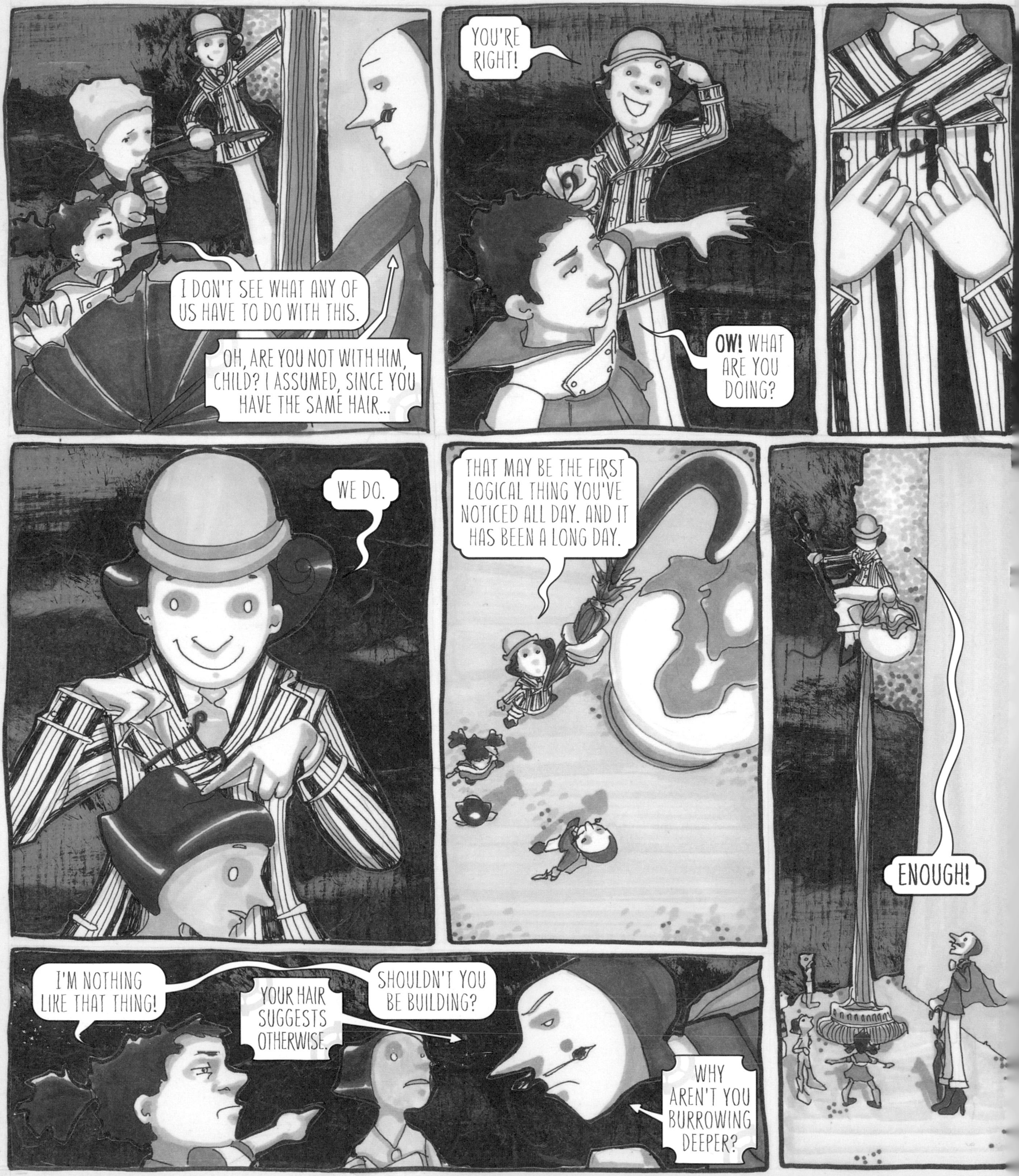
I DON'T SEE WHAT ANY OF US HAVE TO DO WITH THIS.
OH, ARE YOU NOT WITH HIM, CHILD? I ASSUMED, SINCE YOU HAVE THE SAME HAIR...
YOU'RE RIGHT!
OW! WHAT ARE YOU DOING?
WE DO.
THAT MAY BE THE FIRST LOGICAL THING YOU'VE NOTICED ALL DAY. AND IT HAS BEEN A LONG DAY.
ENOUGH!
I'M NOTHING LIKE THAT THING!
YOUR HAIR SUGGESTS OTHERWISE.
SHOULDN'T YOU BE BUILDING?
WHY AREN'T YOU BURROWING DEEPER?

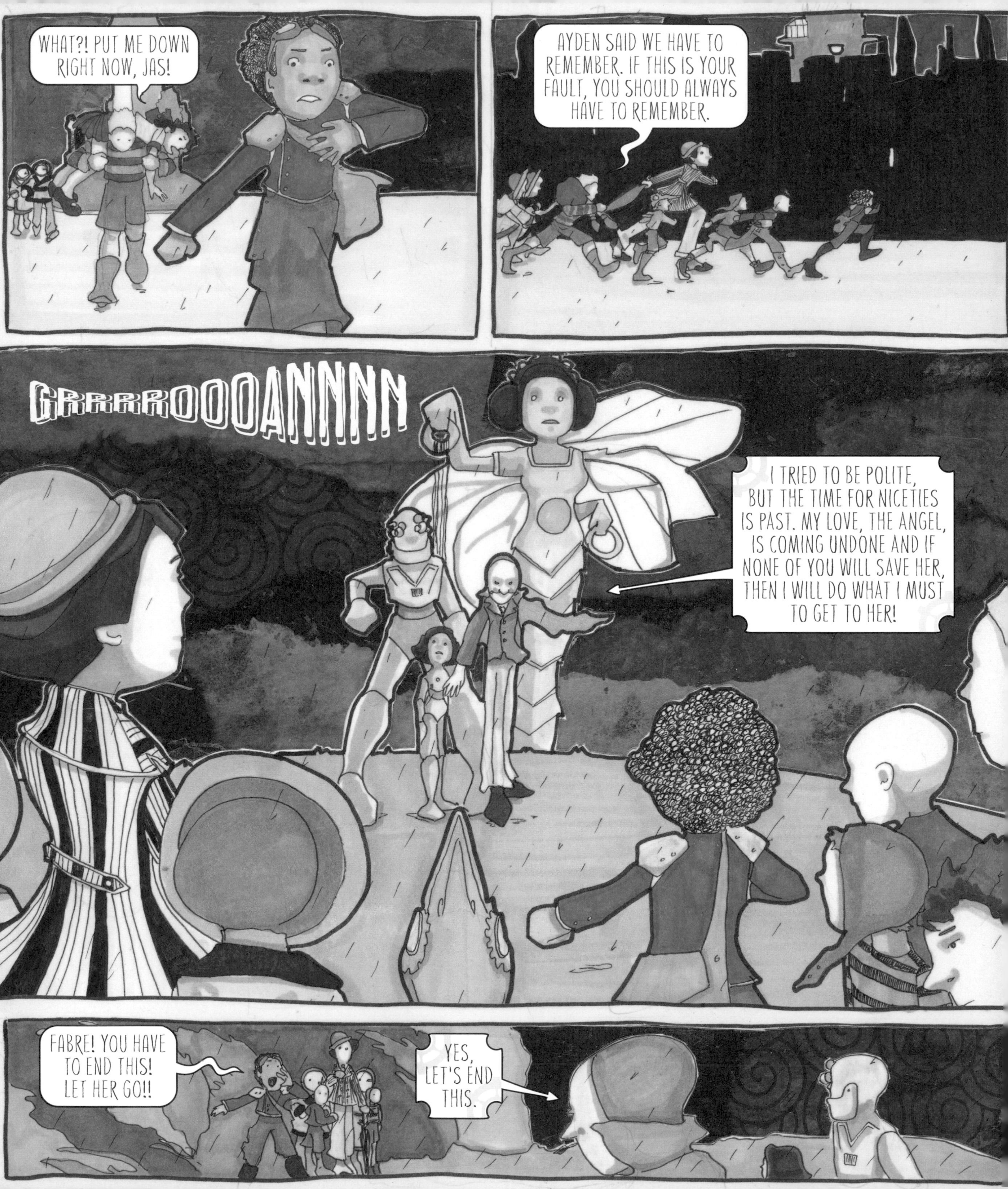
WHAT?! PUT ME DOWN RIGHT NOW, JAS!
AYDEN SAID WE HAVE TO REMEMBER. IF THIS IS YOUR FAULT, YOU SHOULD ALWAYS HAVE TO REMEMBER.
GRRRRROOOOANNNNN
I TRIED TO BE POLITE, BUT THE TIME FOR NICETIES IS PAST. MY LOVE, THE ANGEL, IS COMING UNDONE AND IF NONE OF YOU WILL SAVE HER, THEN I WILL DO WHAT I MUST TO GET TO HER!
FABRE! YOU HAVE TO END THIS! LET HER GO!!
YES, LET'S END THIS.

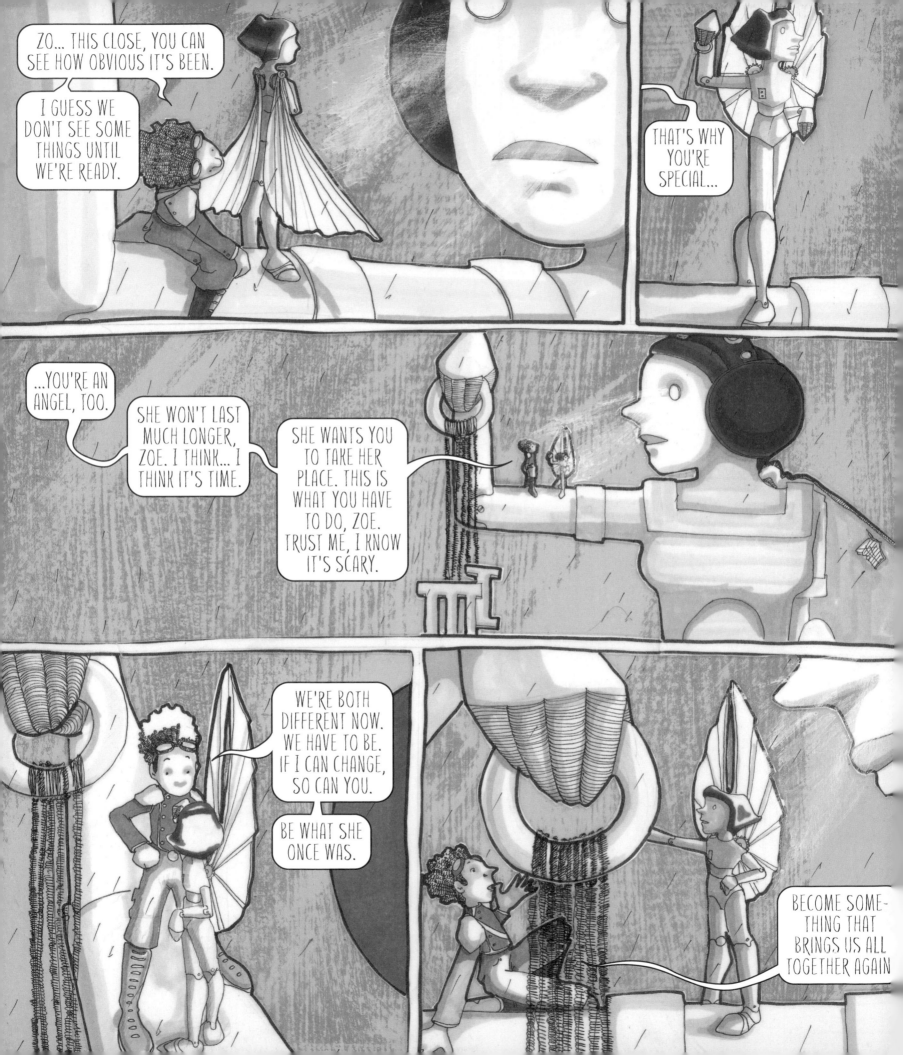

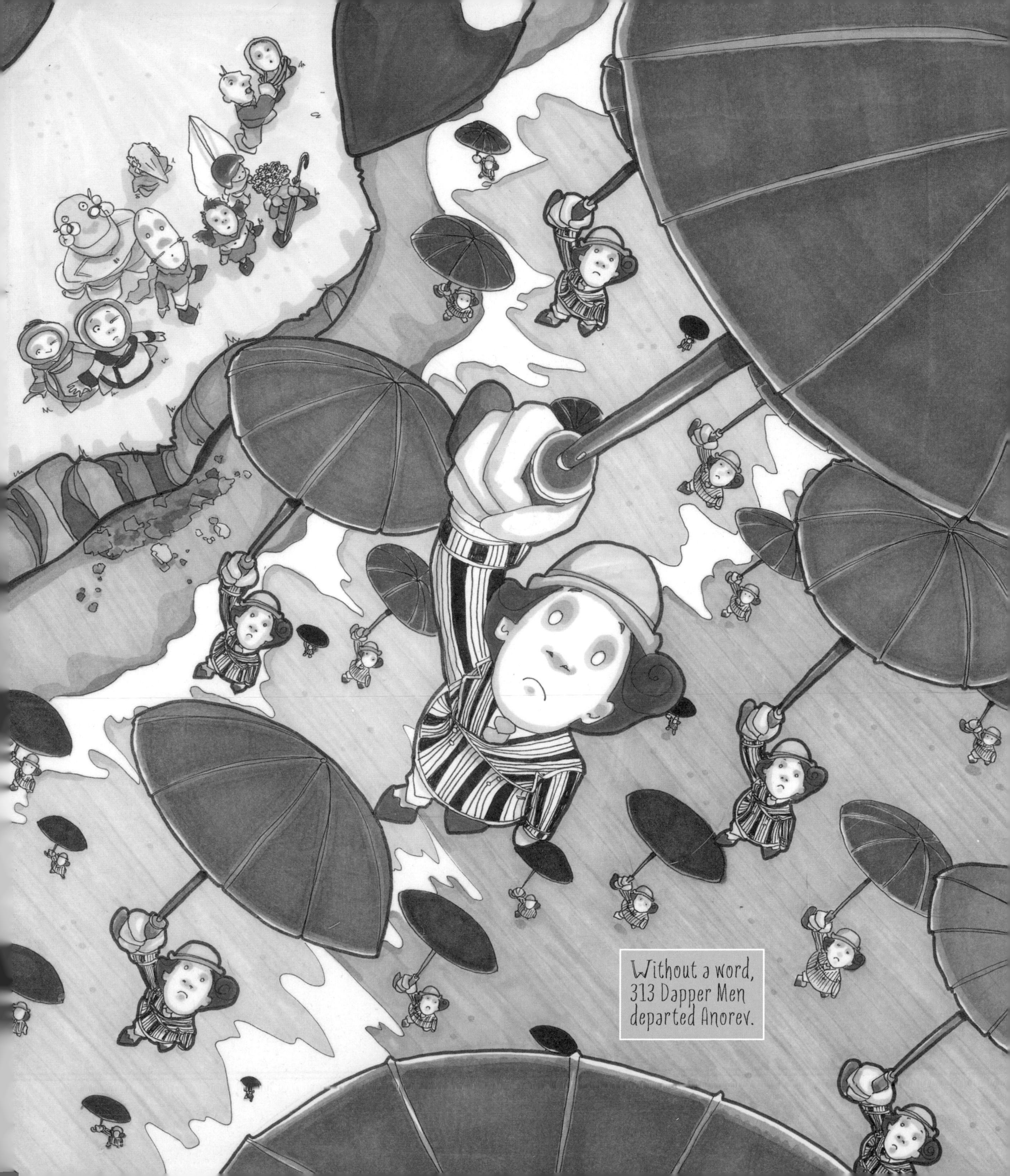
Without a word,
313 Dapper Men
departed Anorev.

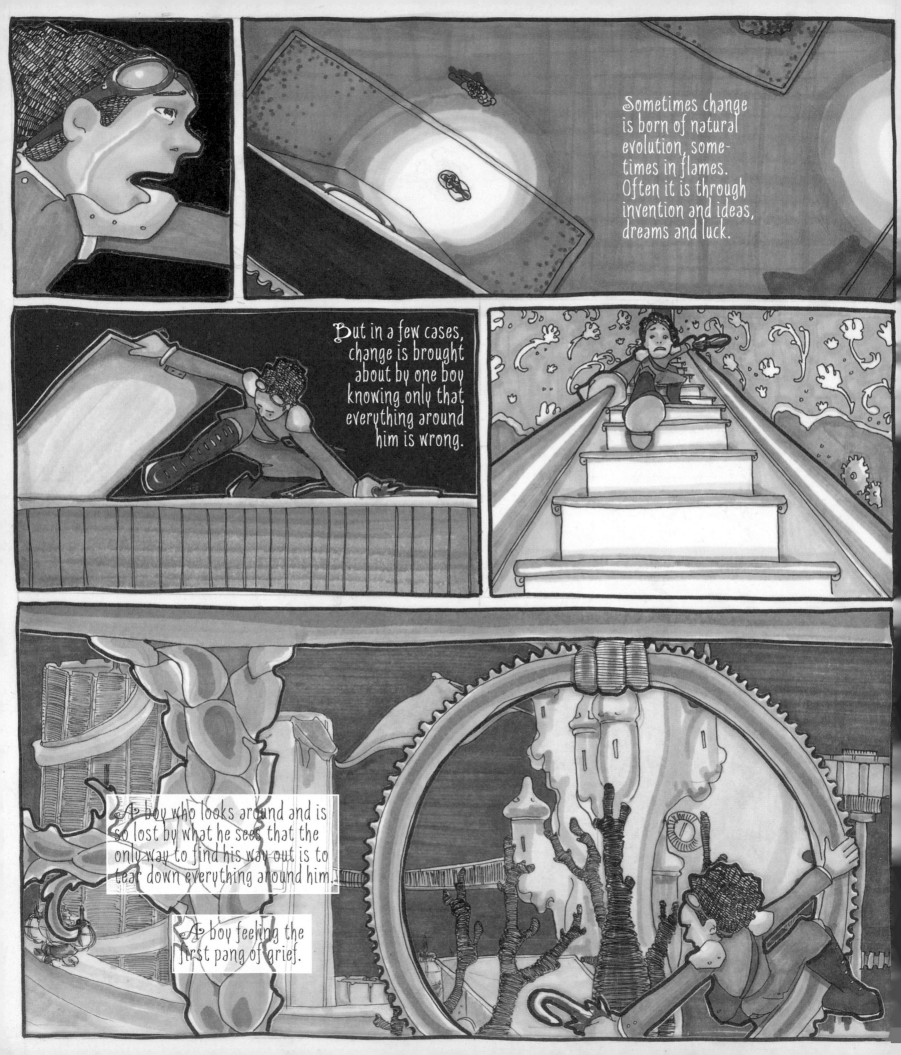

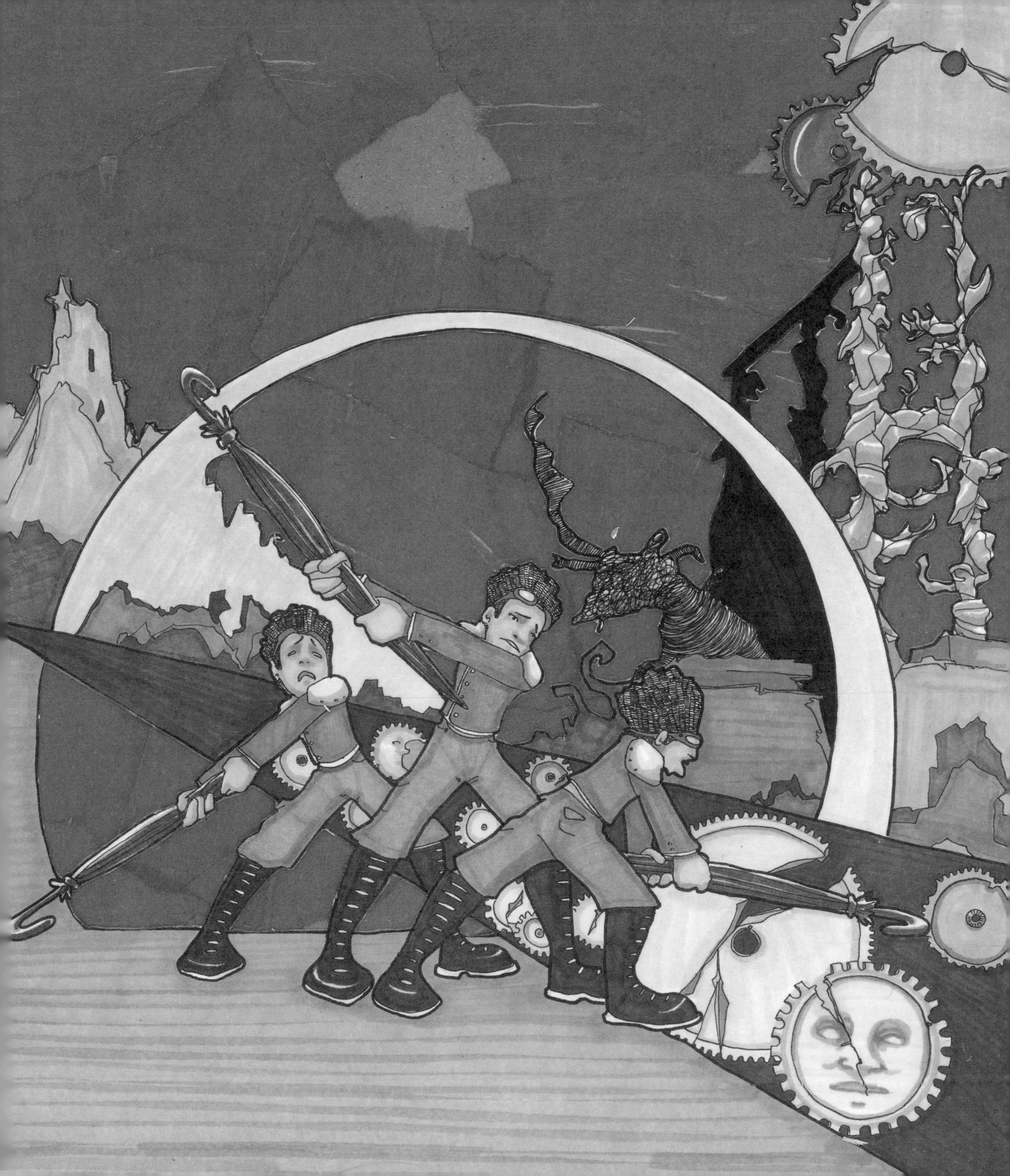

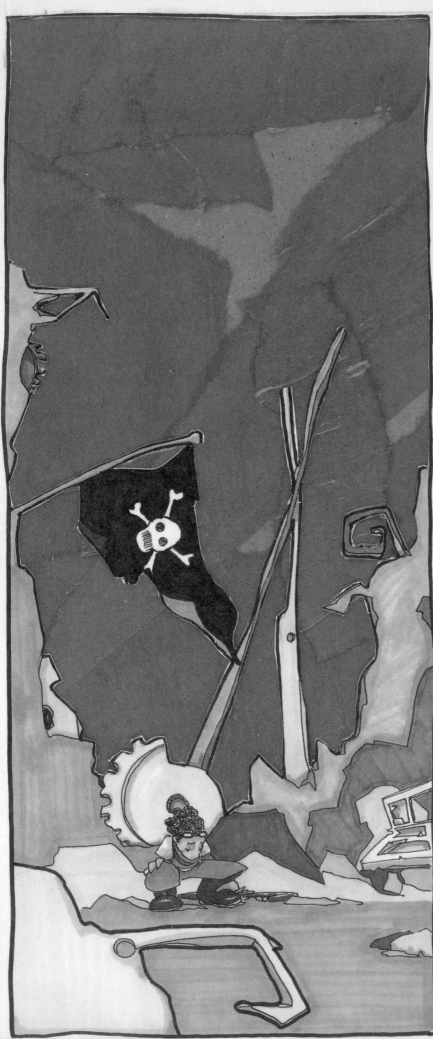

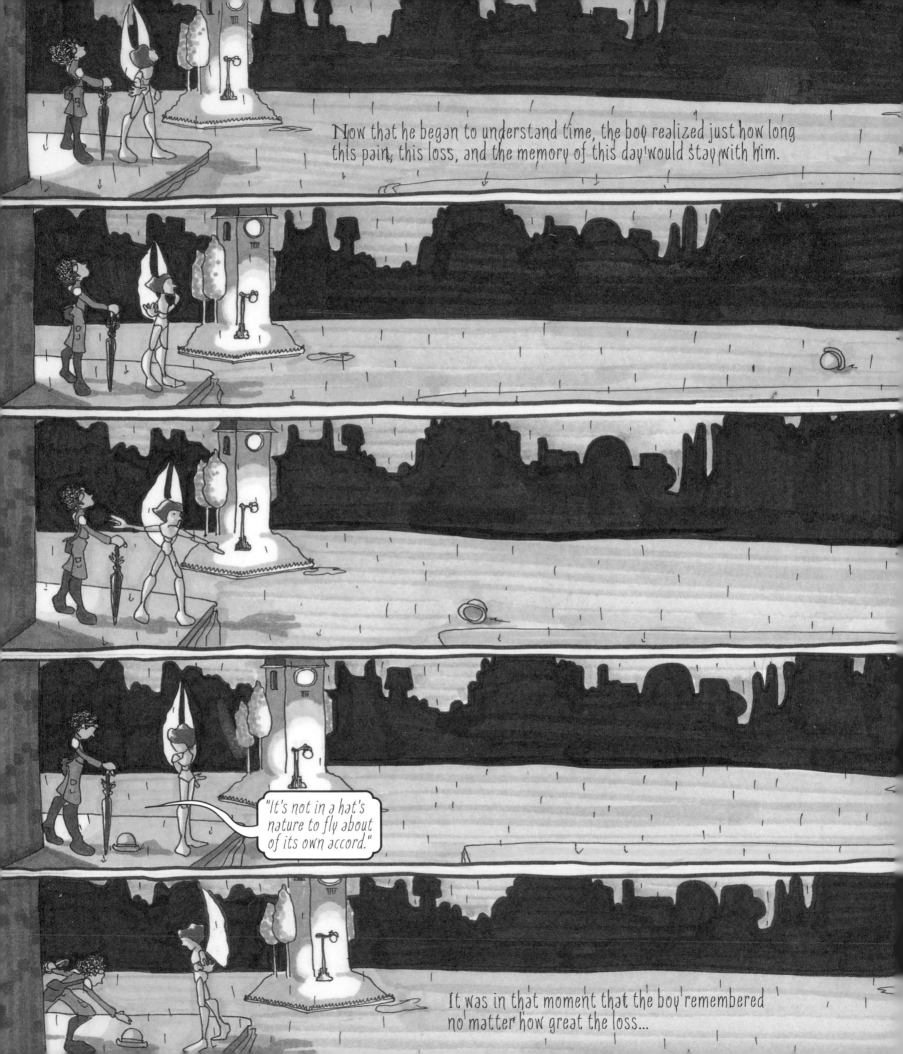

Now that he began to understand time, the boy realized just how long this pain, this loss, and the memory of this day would stay with him.

"It's not in a hat's nature to fly about of its own accord."

It was in that moment that the boy remembered no matter how great the loss...

He would never truly be alone.

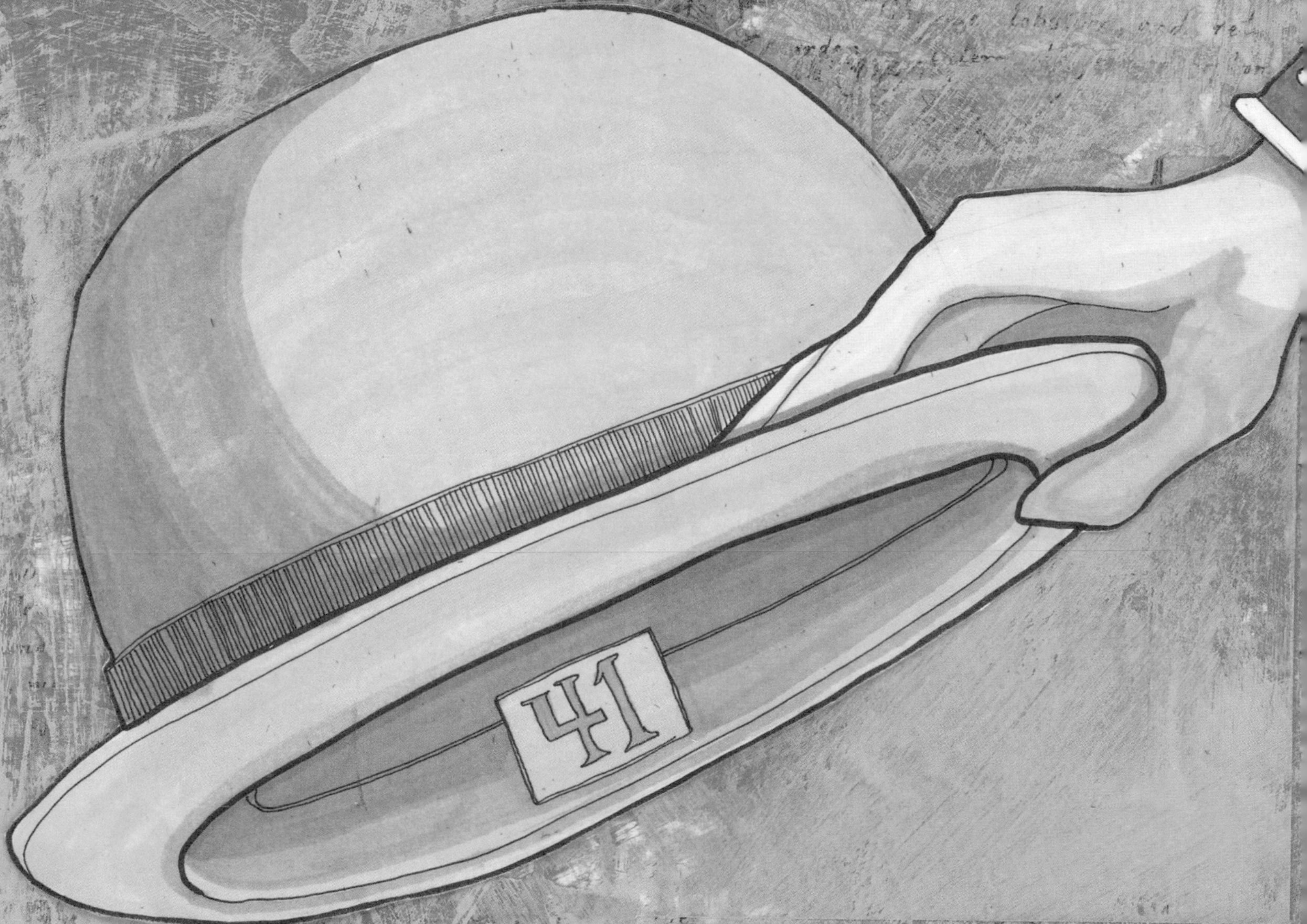

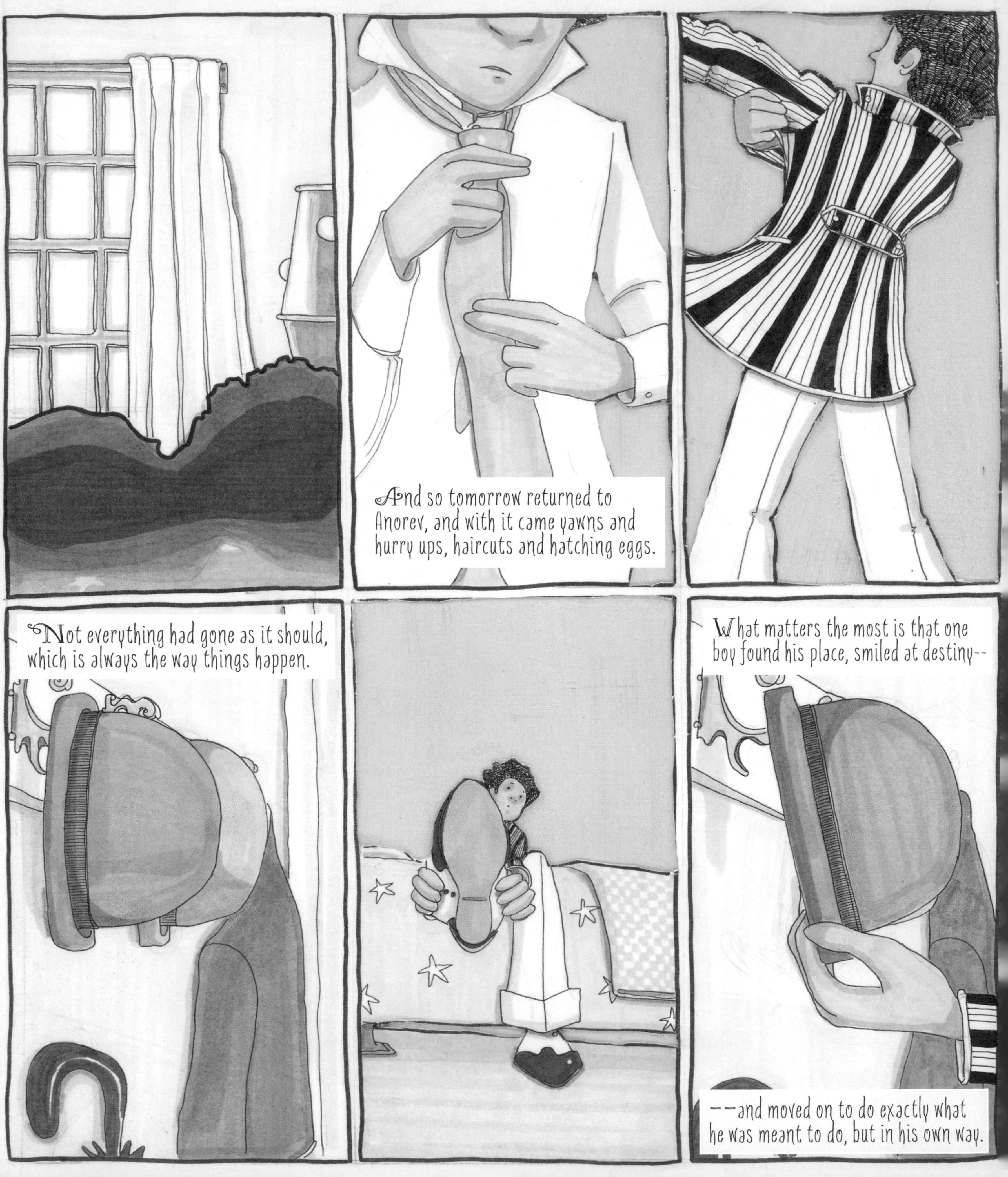
And so tomorrow returned to Anorev, and with it came yawns and hurry ups, haircuts and hatching eggs.
Not everything had gone as it should, which is always the way things happen.
What matters the most is that one boy found his place, smiled at destiny--
--and moved on to do exactly what he was meant to do, but in his own way.

He brought back books, and questions, and changes. He managed to keep his temper to a minimum, focusing on building things rather than tearing them down.

He saw humans and machines dwelling in homes, working together. He witnessed unlikely friends and those he'd rather not see together bond closely.

He saw a change, and he knew it was right. He never forgot to remember.

He saw the world and understood his place in it all.

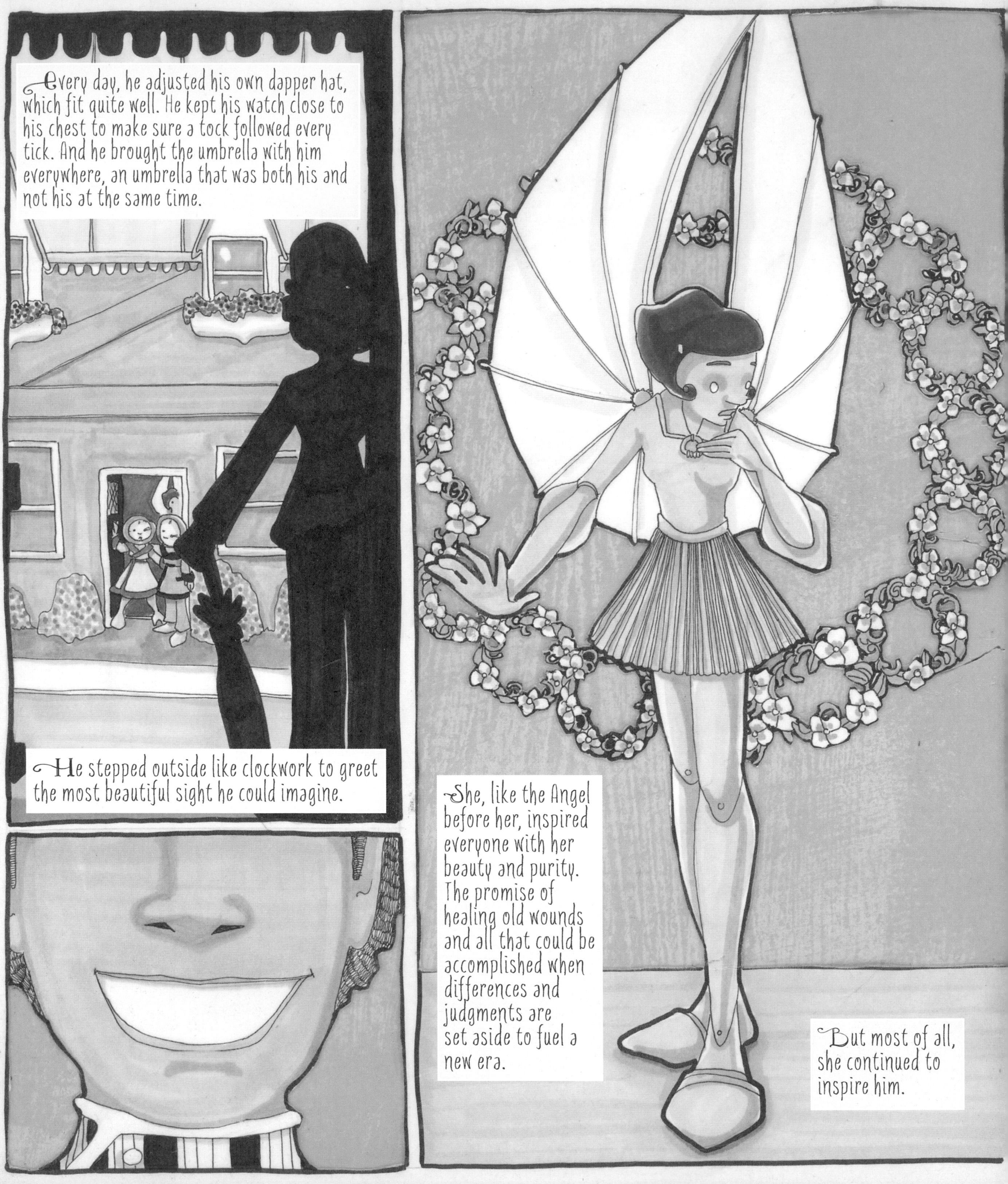
Every day, he adjusted his own dapper hat, which fit quite well. He kept his watch close to his chest to make sure a tock followed every tick. And he brought the umbrella with him everywhere, an umbrella that was both his and not his at the same time.
He stepped outside like clockwork to greet the most beautiful sight he could imagine.
She, like the Angel before her, inspired everyone with her beauty and purity. The promise of healing old wounds and all that could be accomplished when differences and judgments are set aside to fuel a new era.
But most of all, she continued to inspire him.

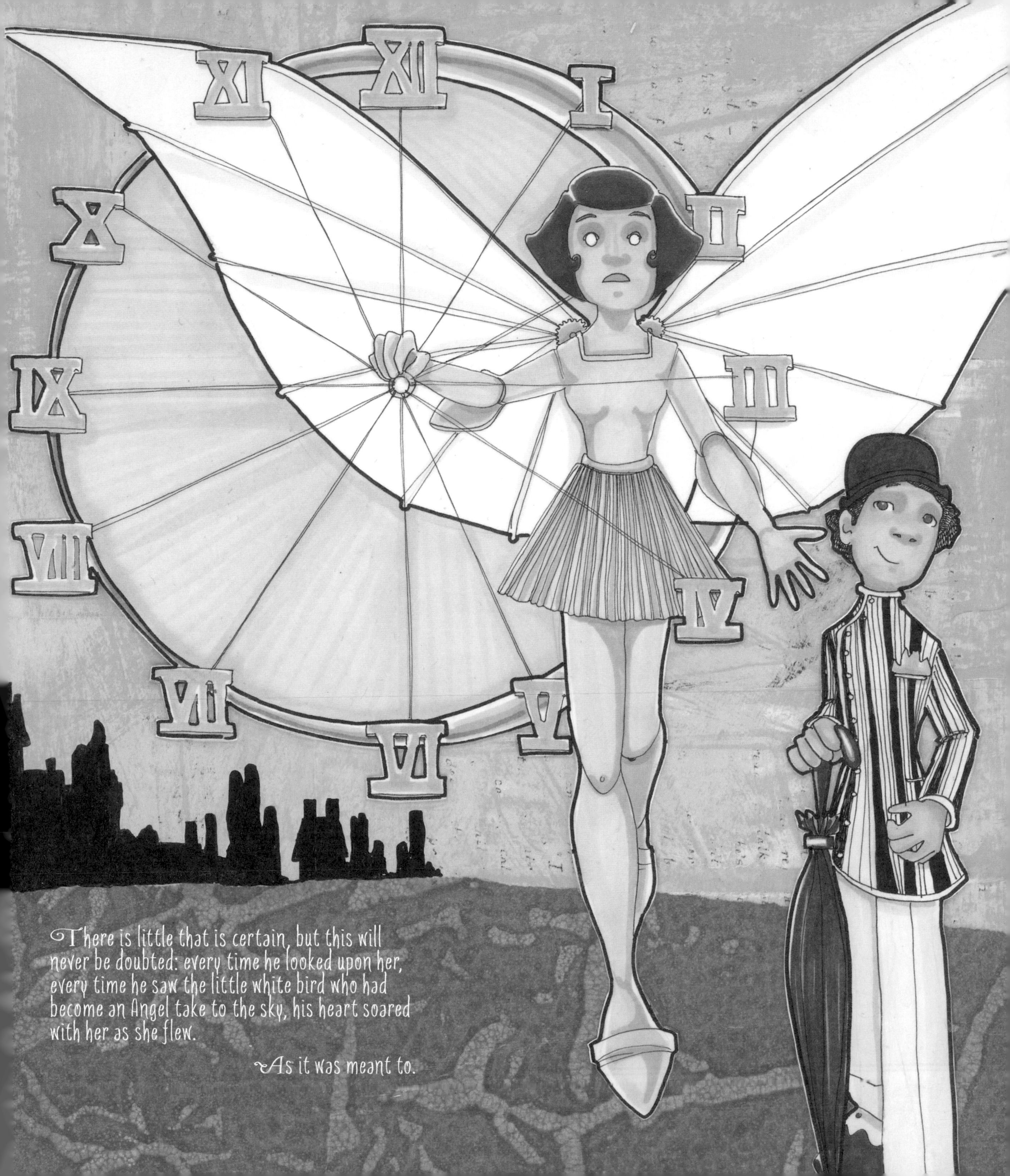

There is little that is certain, but this will never be doubted: every time he looked upon her, every time he saw the little white bird who had become an Angel take to the sky, his heart soared with her as she flew.

As it was meant to.

And there was, as it happened, always time for a nice cup of warm tea.

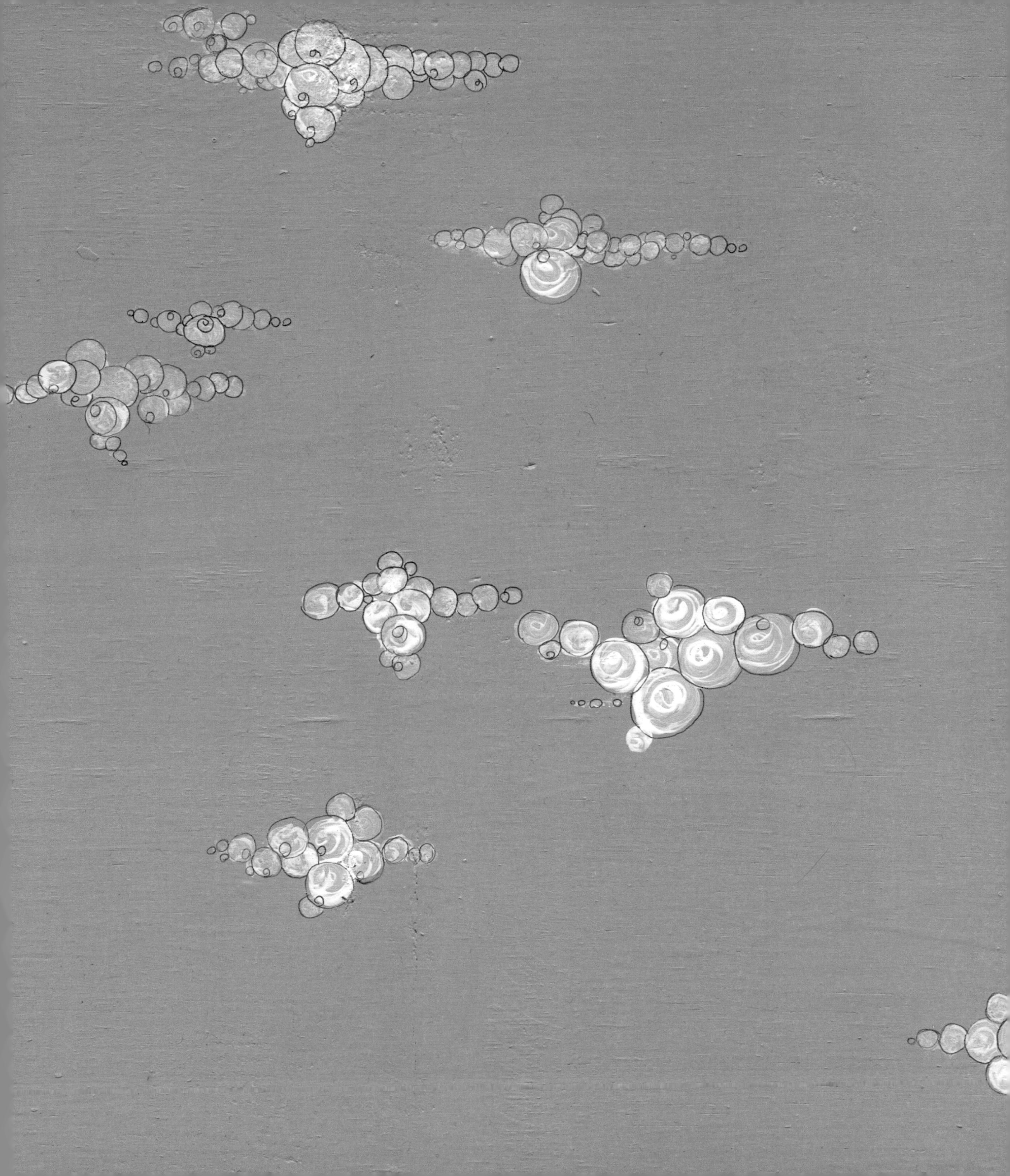

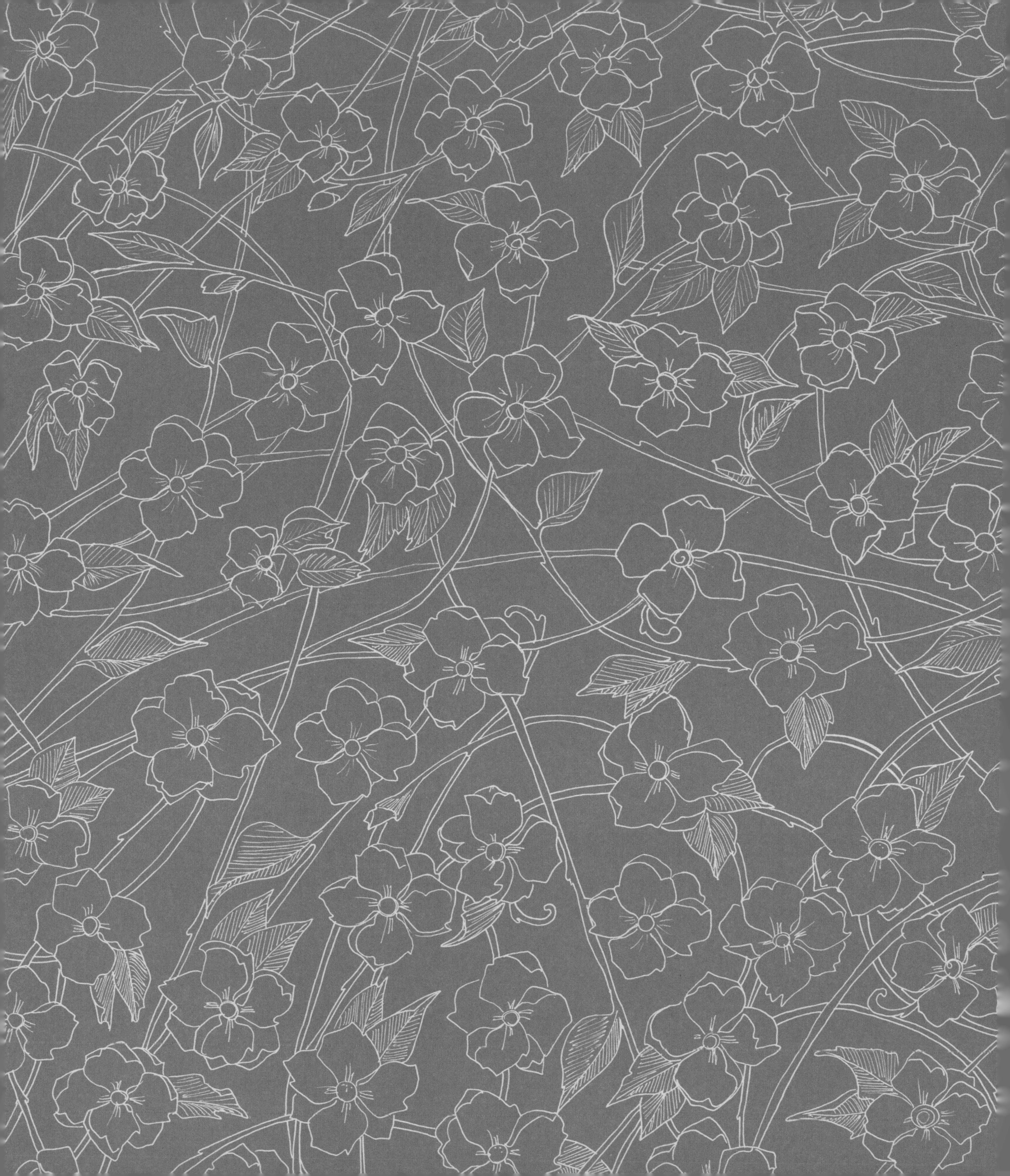

A GALLERY OF ART BY ESTEEMED COLLEAGUES AND FRIENDS

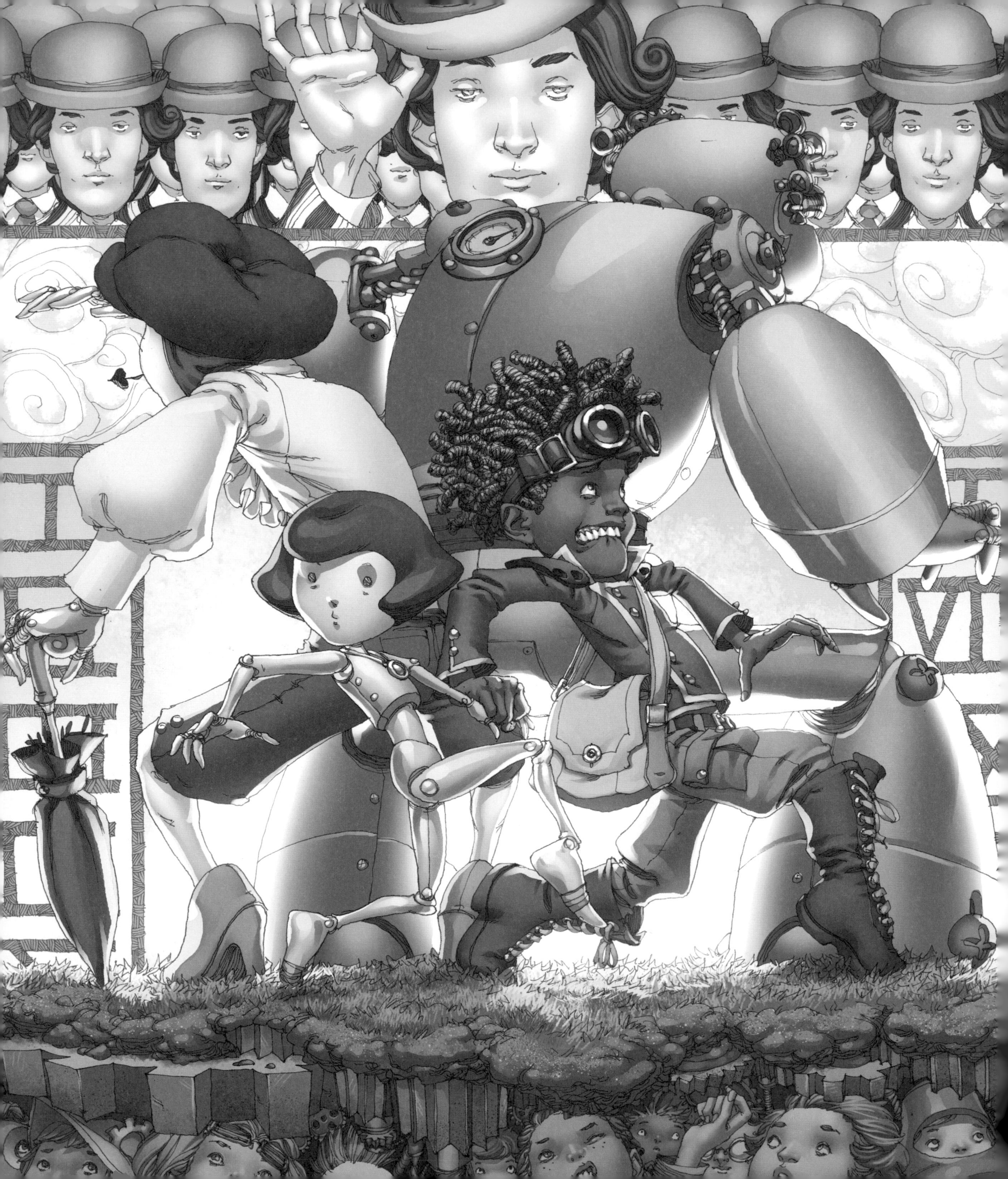

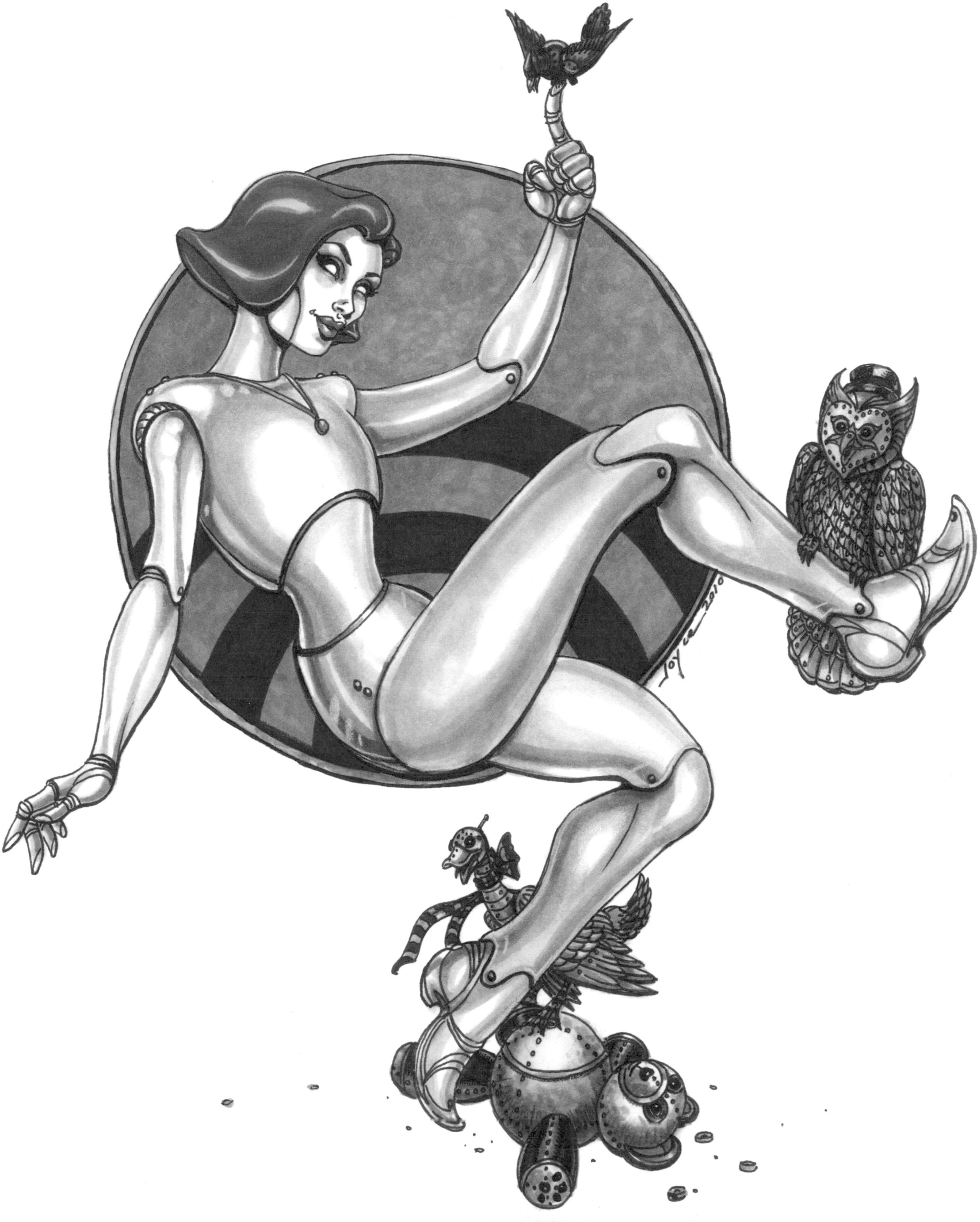
Joyce 2010

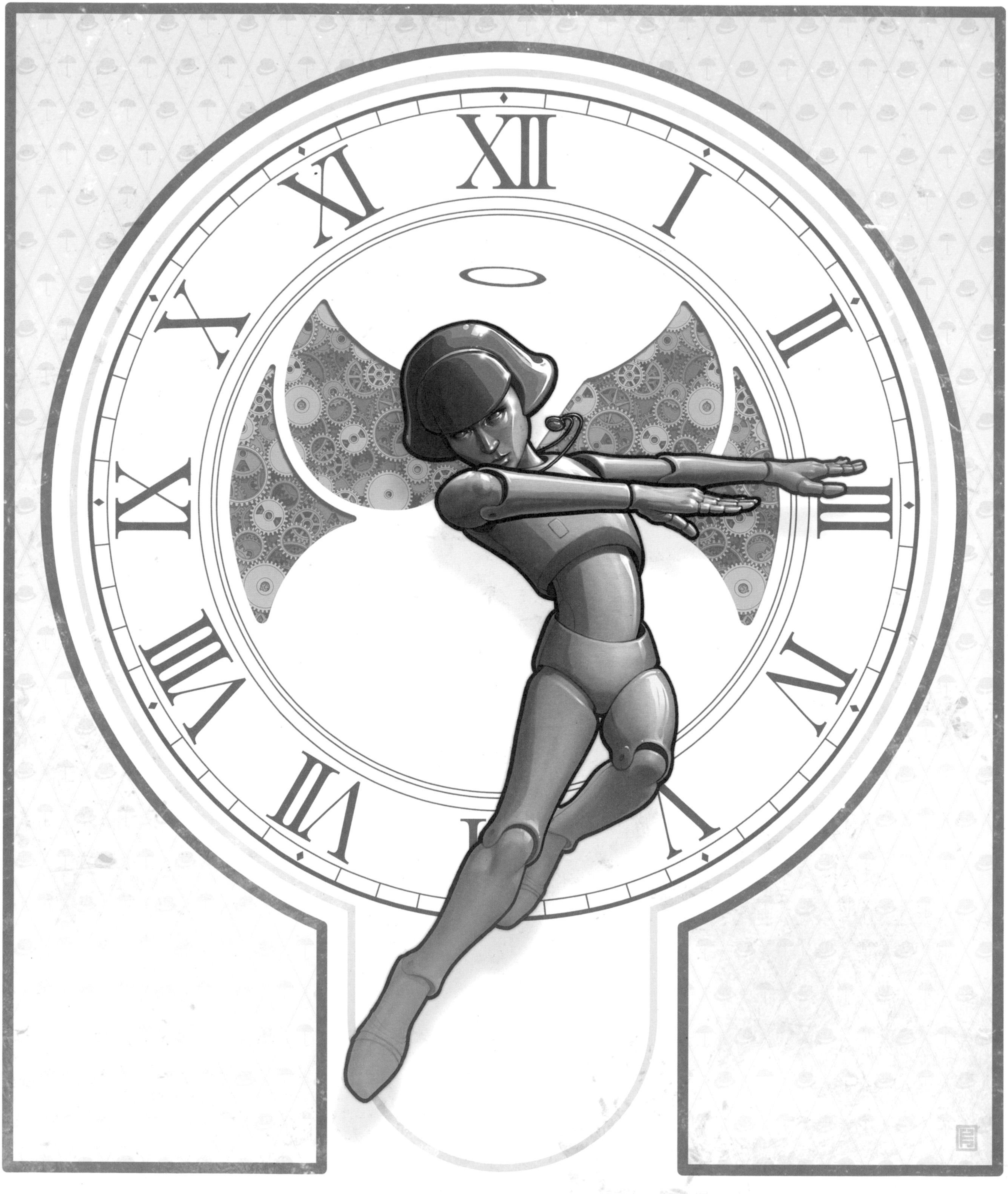

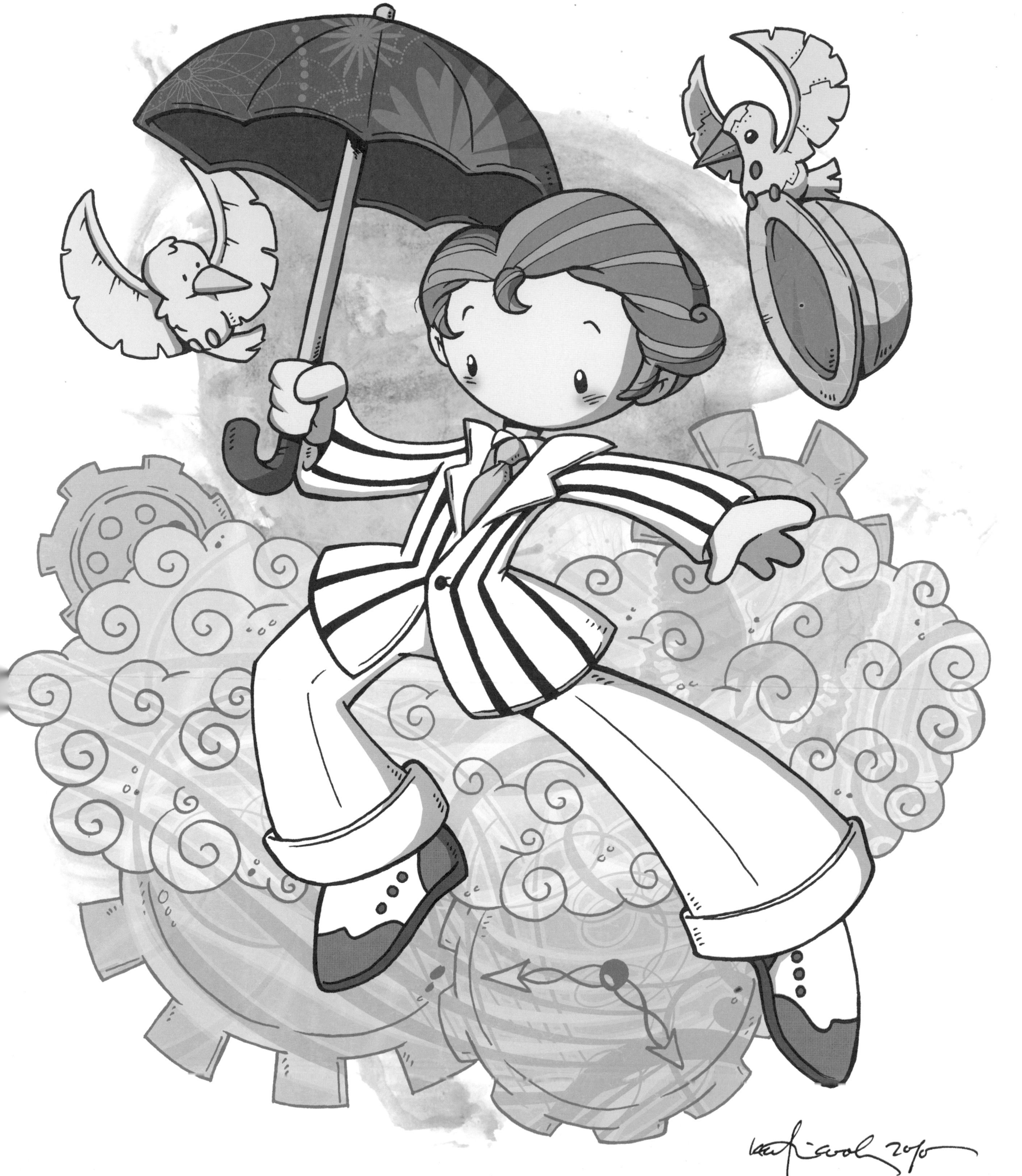

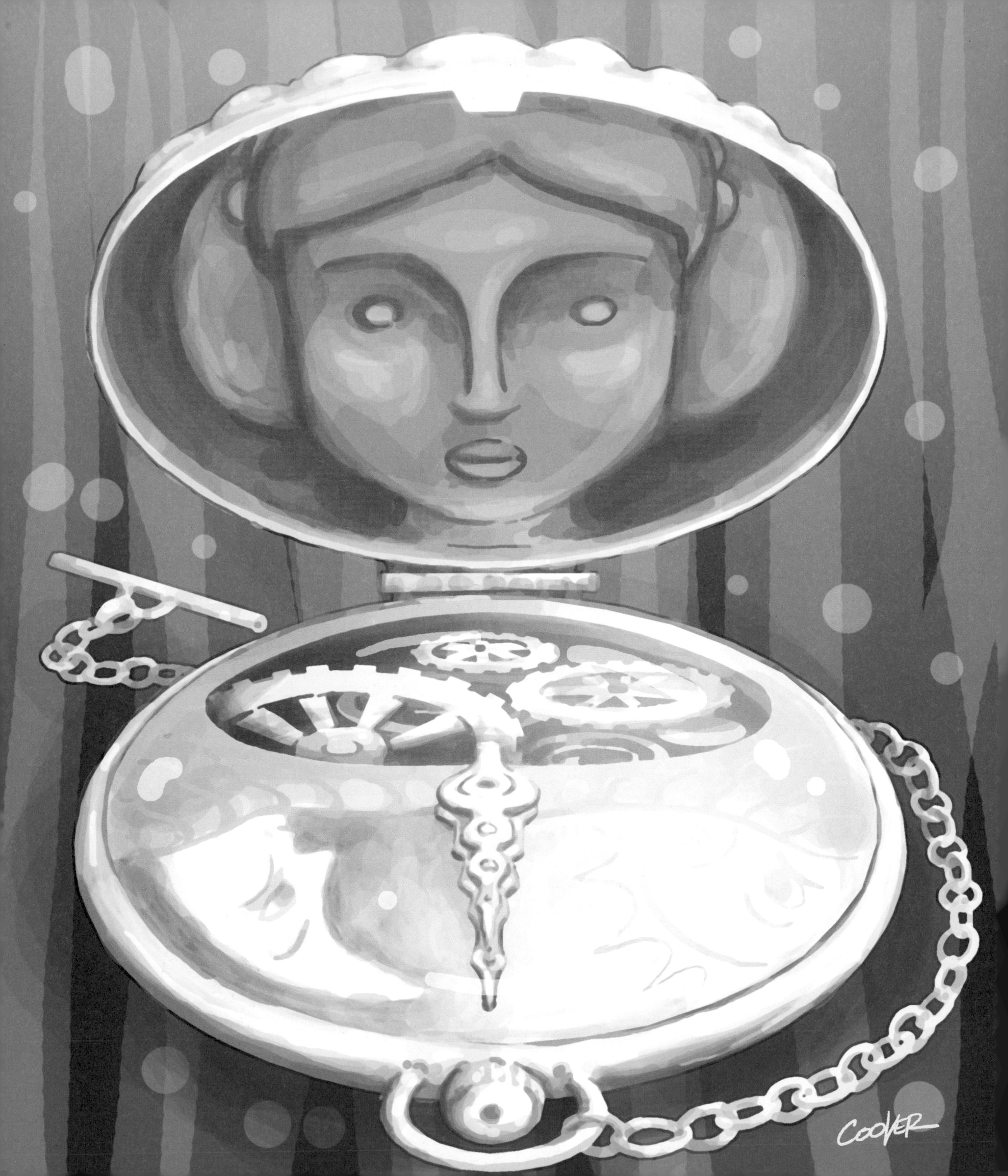
COOVER

babtistes Well.
comming up for Gir from Brooklyn in the 1yr
overwhelmed w tears of
I drank tea I did'nt dately beautifuL luminescent
now for one of my Spectacular looked like a pearl
Find a Sequence of discourse clusters & I was treated
say his name FeeL terribly ancestraL
a child of the Leaves
they are famous adventu
I can hard fathom how
Scarred Broken
strange. Who
So I think this is a bit
hopefully not
I have a new face
creeping my peculiar progr

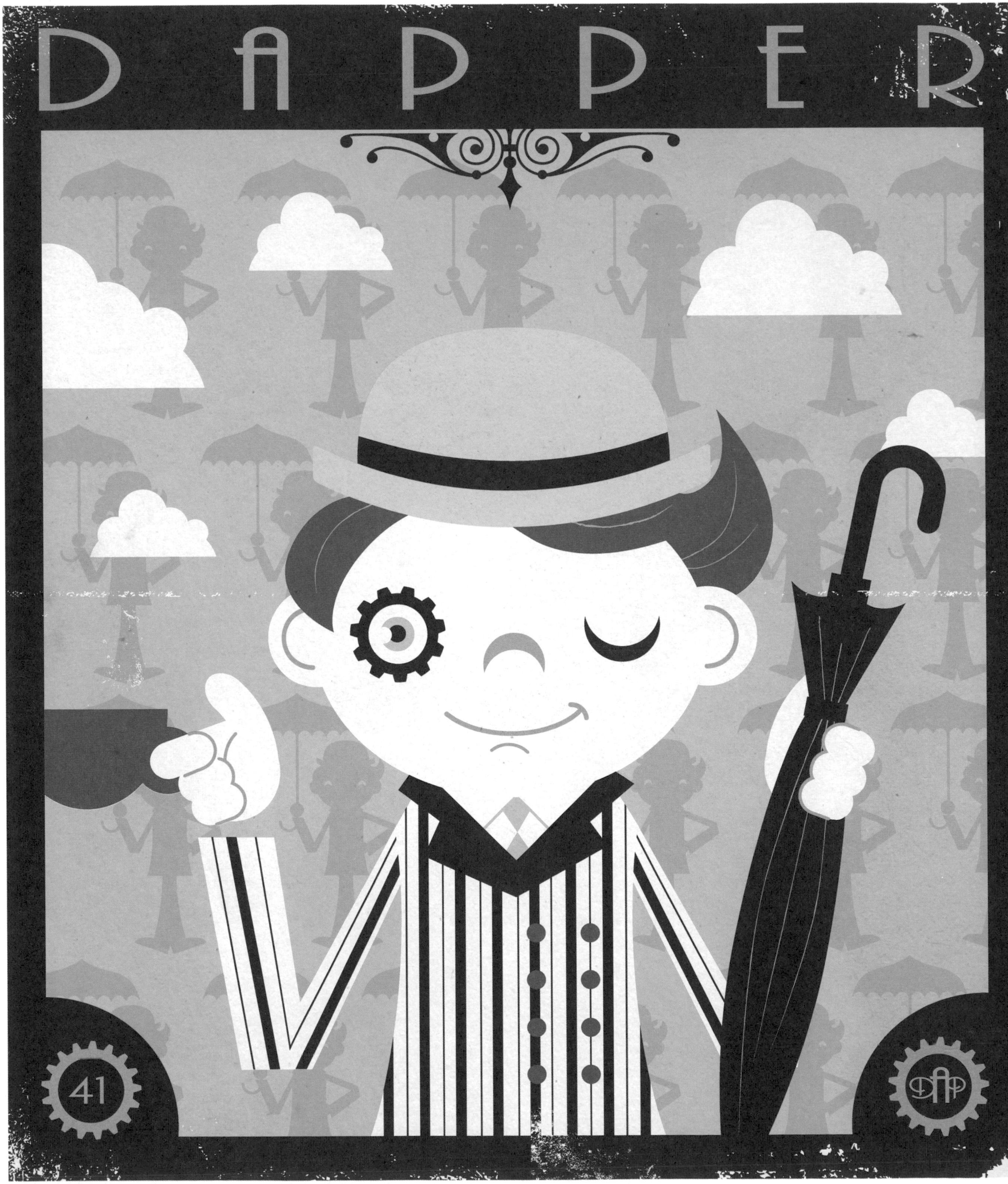
DAPPER
41
DAP

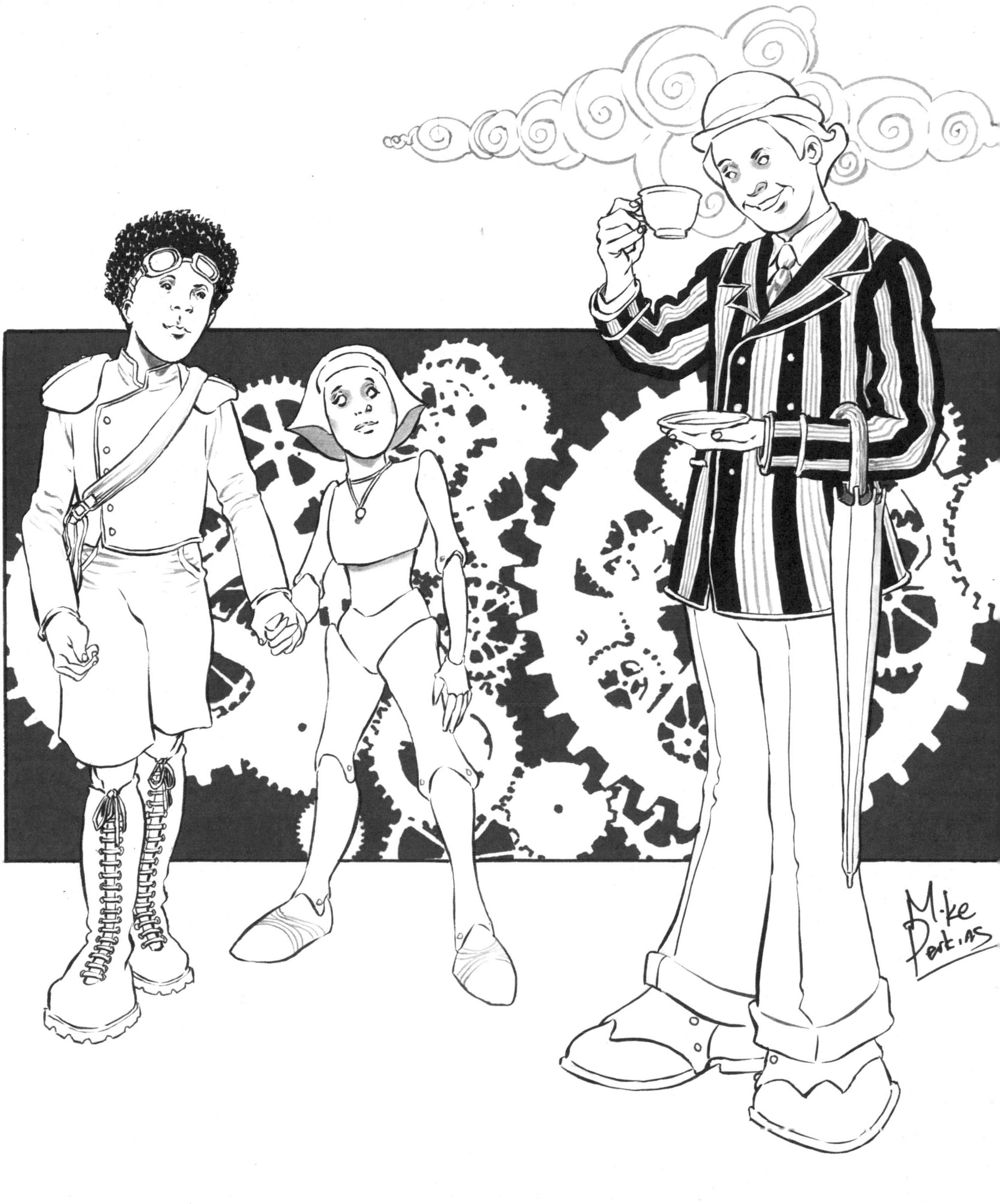
Mike Perkins

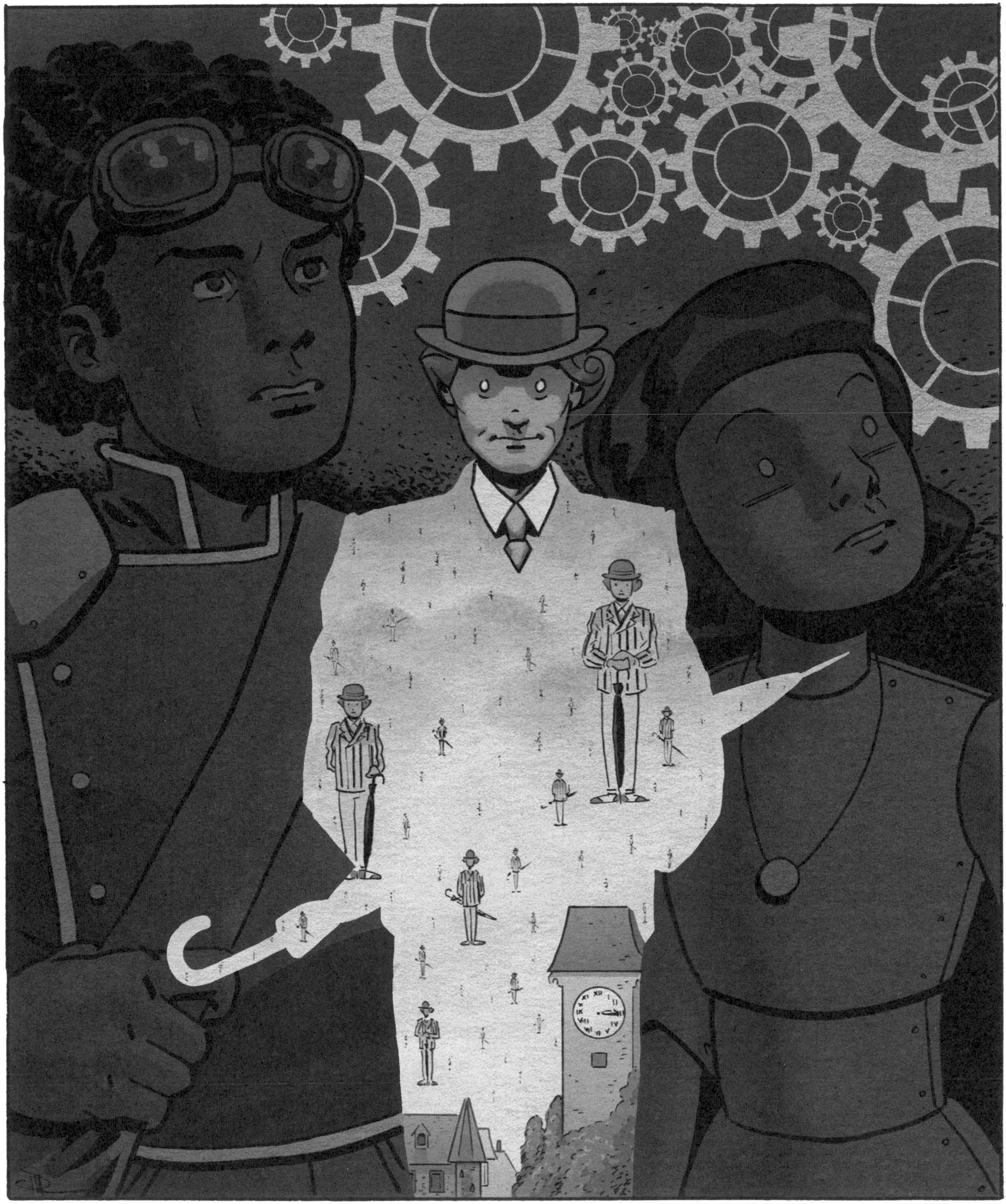

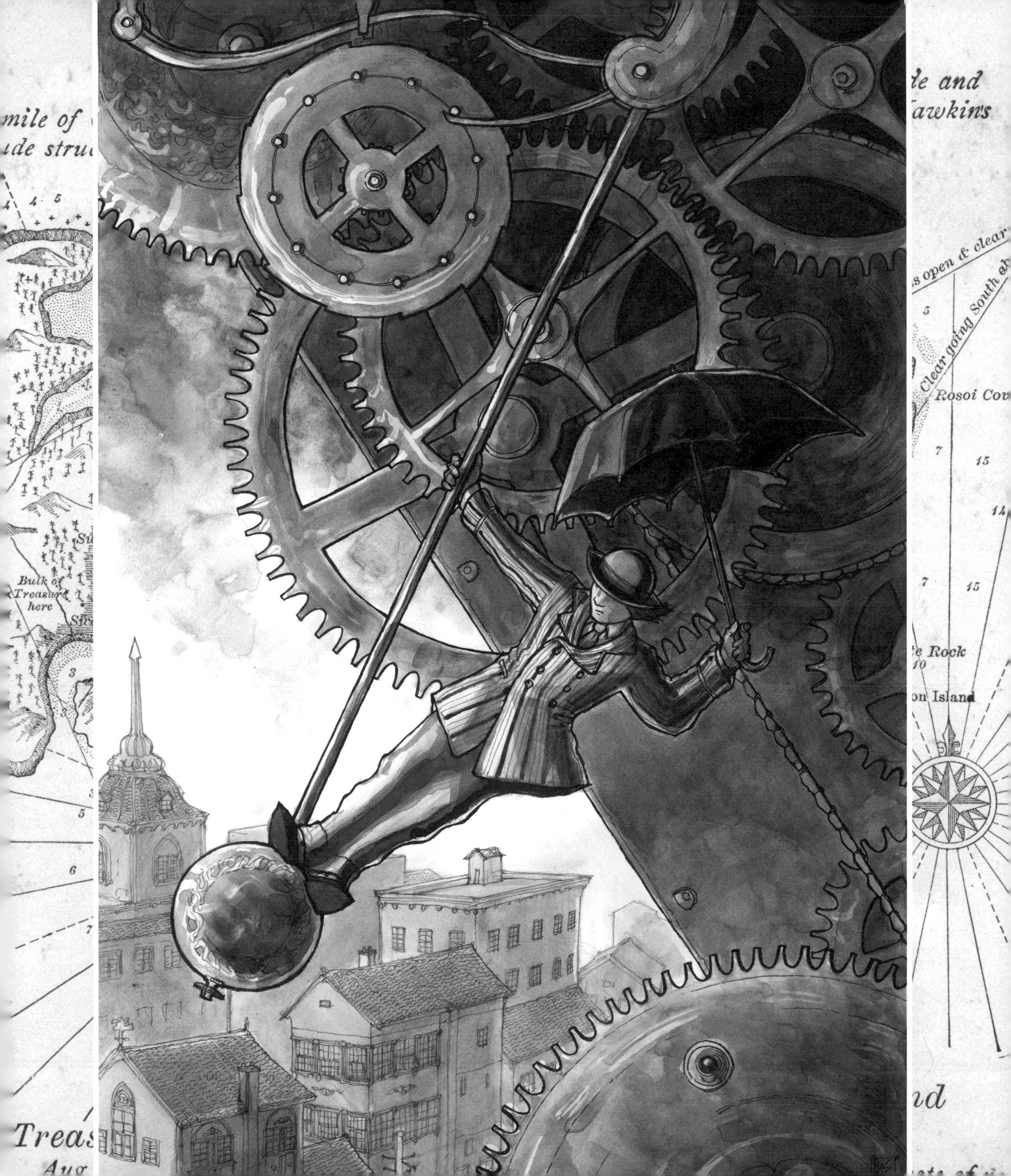

mile of
Bulk of
here
Clear going South
Rosoi Cov
Rock
Island

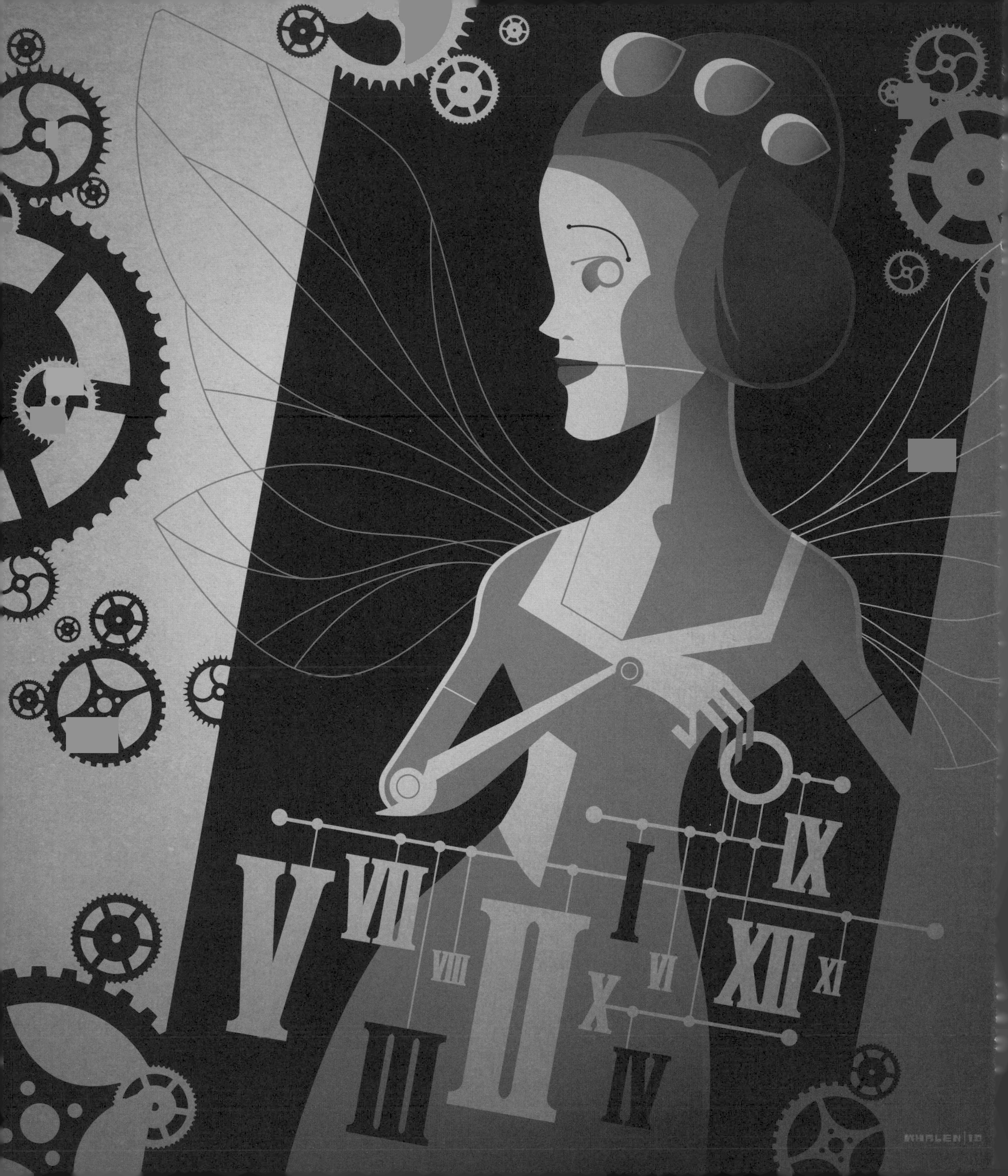
V
VII
I
IX
VIII
II
VI
X
XII
XI
III
IV
WHALEN|10

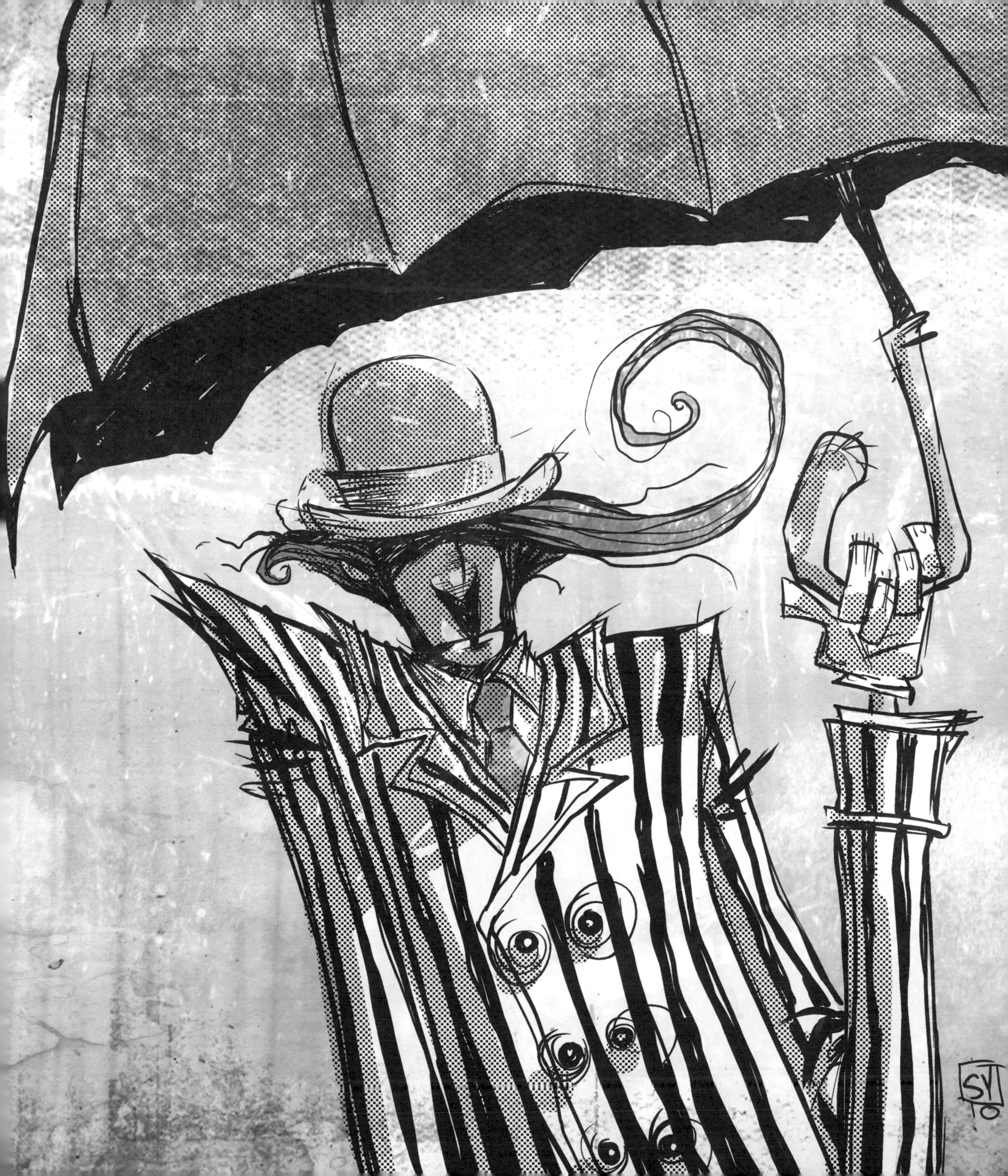

THE MAKING OF A DAPPER PAGE

One of the things that has continued to catch people's attention about *RETURN OF THE DAPPER MEN,* from the initial pitch to convention appearances to the final book has been the art. Not only because of its imaginative style and inspirational visuals, but because of the actual art itself, specifically *how* the art was made. Janet's process has been called "groundbreaking" and "revolutionary," but it's rooted in a time-honored tradition: decoupage. It's this style that adds texture and depth to an already rich world, giving it an organic feel in a world comprised of robots and pin-stripe suits.

So, how does she do it?

The construction of a page begins with the script. Janet and I have known each other for years and it was her art style that inspired the fairy tale approach to the story of *RETURN OF THE DAPPER MEN.* Janet, being a gallery artist, could handle a number of splash pages with very little direction — in fact, for many of them, I would indicate in the script the general feeling that we were going for and provided the narration and let her go free. This, however, was her first graphic novel, which meant she needed to take her style and adopt it to sequential visual storytelling. It also meant I had to adjust a bit as well. As we got deeper into the story and Janet became more comfortable with the sequential pages and multiple panels, I started adding more. It also fit the theme of the book-that Time had returned and order was being restored. It also helped drive home the urgency as the sun was setting. This urgency came to a head in page 70.

Here is the script for page 70:

PAGE 70

Panel 1: *41 is looking up among the clouds.*
41: We can't be everywhere at once. Well, we could, I suppose, but that's neither here nor there. Or there. Or even way out there.

Panel 2: *He turns towards the crowd (and us).*
41: The point is we shouldn't have needed to return! But you...you just stopped! Does it matter where we've been when it's you who should have been going places?

Panels 3 - 8: *A series of small panels (like when Fabre was trying on hats) with Harmony and Jas, Devick & Dear, Fabre & Guillaume, Reese and Dak and Llew, Zoe and Ayden all taking it in in their own way (Fabre, eyebrow cocked, Devick & Dear huddled together, Harm's arms crossed, Ayden and Zoe understanding), silent. The last small panel should be filled with four Dappers, just looking, with their frowns.*

Panel 9: *A small panel of 41, looking down.*
41: I know...I've already said too much.

Panel 10: *Ayden steps forward to address the group. 41 is looking up, a proud look in his eye.*
AYDEN: He's right. Everything's wrong. Look around us.
AYDEN: We forgot to remember.

Panel 11: *Strip across the page. The other Dappers turn away as Ayden and 41 start to walk. In the background, Harmony and Fabre are sizing each other up. Devick and Dear are with Zoe. 41 is moving Ayden off by himself.*
Silence.

We wanted to show as many of the major characters as possible in this moment. 41 understands that he can only say so much, that those who inhabit Anorev need to learn for themselves again. But he has a very captive audience, from the kids to the robots and even some of the other Dapper Men. This was the turning point, the moment we'd start entering ACT III. Ayden finished what 41 started to say, just as it was his destiny to continue everything that 41 left behind.

I knew this would be a difficult page, having 11 panels on the page, but Janet had a great grasp of perspective and character grouping for those

middle panels. And so she started, as most artists do, by drawing.

Janet uses Strathmore Bristol Vellum paper, a slightly texturized and heavy stock paper. She pencils and scans those pencils for me to review. Once approved, which this page was immediately, she goes on to inks, using a combination of Faber and Cassell brush pens and Micron .005 pens. The heavy black lines indicate what will be cut after coloring.

For coloring, she used a wide variety of Prismacolor markers. To achieve the proper shine and texture, multiple hues of the same color are often needed. Fun fact (for the reader, not as much fun for Janet): the hair for the Dapper Men has five different shades of red/orange to achieve that glow and shine. Another fact, one that was pointed out by 41 in the book, is that Zoe's hair is colored using the same five hues as the Dapper Men. Harmony's hair only uses four of the hues.

cut outs. Those panels had the backgrounds cut out so that the sunset on the painted wood would catch your eye and remind you that the world around them is changing.

Next up is painting the board. Each of these pages are mounted on board, usually pine, which Janet buys from the lumber section of her local home improvement store, and then takes to the basement and cuts to approximately trim size using a power saw. She sometimes uses pages from books, art papers, or designs that she's drawn to lay down a background on the pine. Usually, as in this page, she paints the wood whatever background color the scene requires, using mistints of house paint, also found at the home improvement store. In this case, the sun is setting and change is in the air, so she painted it using the base coat of the cerulean blue that the Dapper Men had brought back to the world when Time started again and ten layers of sunset colors. Knowing that there would be multiple pages like this, she painted a few boards at a time, then let them dry.

Laying down the layers, Janet then uses a popular item from the 1970s — Mod Podge — to glue the layers to the board. Once the layers are in place and glued down, a varnish is applied to seal the entire thing. Janet has said that her method was developed to make her art kid-proof, going so far as to say you could tap dance on it if you wanted to. The only thing to avoid is getting the piece wet. As you can see, the finished page is also a ready-to-hang piece of gallery art. The board is scanned in high res, the excess is cropped, the lettering layered, and there you have it — a finished page of a graphic novel, done unlike any other that I've seen.

While the backgrounds drying, it's time to cut. Using three different types of scissors, she goes in and cuts out everywhere that the background should be seen. In other pages, she would sometimes draw additional characters on another page, cut them out, and use them as a layer. In this case, however, it was 41 and the message he started and Ayden continues that were the most important panels, so those were the ones that had the

It's an unusual approach and one that has evolved as we put together this first book, all of us learning along the way. But it is one that has inspired me from the moment I saw the three art pieces she had done over various times during Christmas, 2008, that would eventually spark the idea of *RETURN OF THE DAPPER MEN* in my mind. Janet has jokingly dismissed her process as a "poor-man's Photoshop," but I think I speak for everyone that sees her work in person and now on the printed page when I say, we're all a little richer for experiencing her art.

Jim McCann, September, 2010

ABOUT THE CREATORS

Jim McCann is an award-winning writer of stage, television, and comic books. Before he could write, he found himself swept away by fairy tales in books and movies. He lived in Nashville, TN, but spent most of his time in galaxies far, far away. He wrote his first short story at the age of ten and hasn't looked back. Eventually he moved to the fairy tale city of New York where he fulfilled a childhood dream and life-long goal — working for Marvel Comics - where he stayed for six years before leaping off the sidewalk's end into the land of full-time writing. Anorev, the land in RETURN OF THE DAPPER MEN, is the biggest world he's ever visited and hopes everyone feels welcome to take their shoes off and escape to whenever they want.

When **Janet Lee** was a child, she couldn't decide if she wanted to be a singer, an actor, a writer, or an artist. She stopped acting after high school. She stopped singing after studying Opera. She got a degree in British Literature from a near-ivy-league college and worked for more than a decade in the book industry, but she never wrote a novel. Through it all she never stopped drawing and making things and telling stories with her art. In time, she showed her artwork in galleries around her hometown of Nashville and was acclaimed by local critics. One day, her friend Jim McCann called to ask Janet if she would illustrate a wonderful book called Return of the Dapper Men—which she had always wanted to do even before she knew the question. And she did!

Time cannot show favor or weep. Time can slow to allow you to savor moments, and can help old wounds heal. But most of all, it lets you know when you have to move on...

TIME of the DAPPER MEN

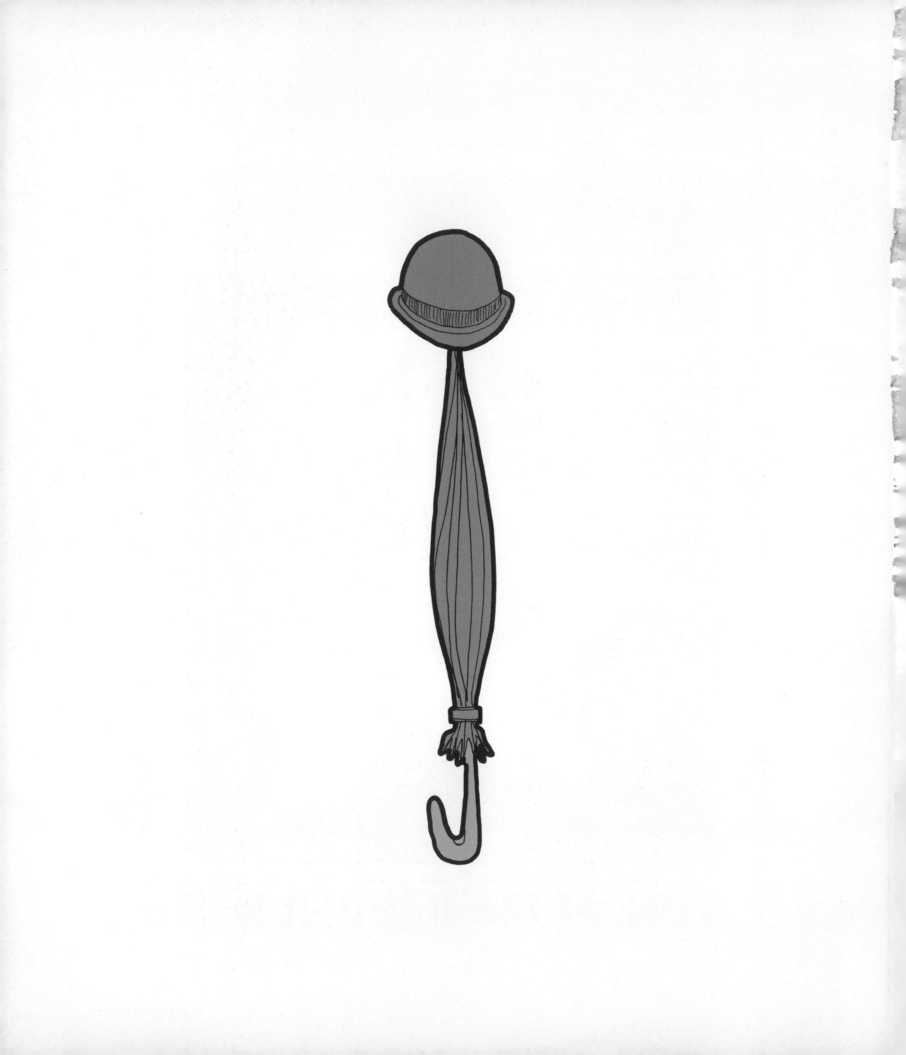

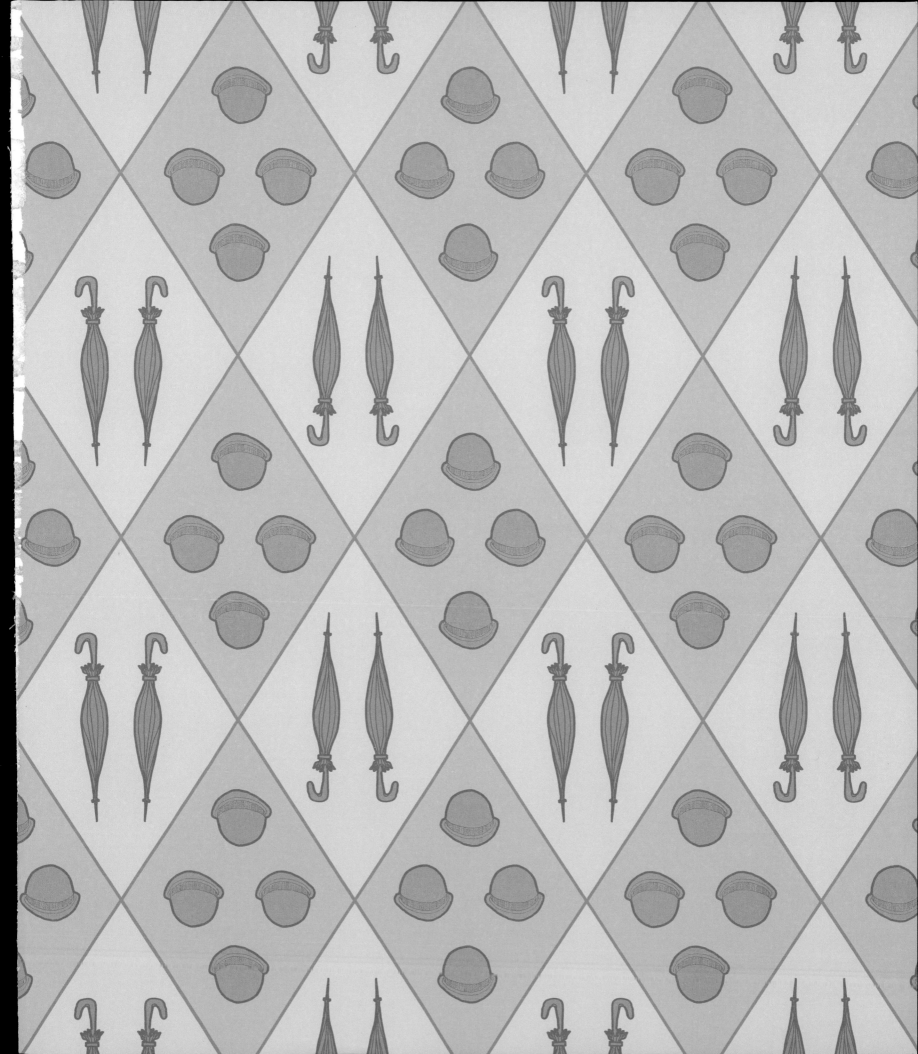

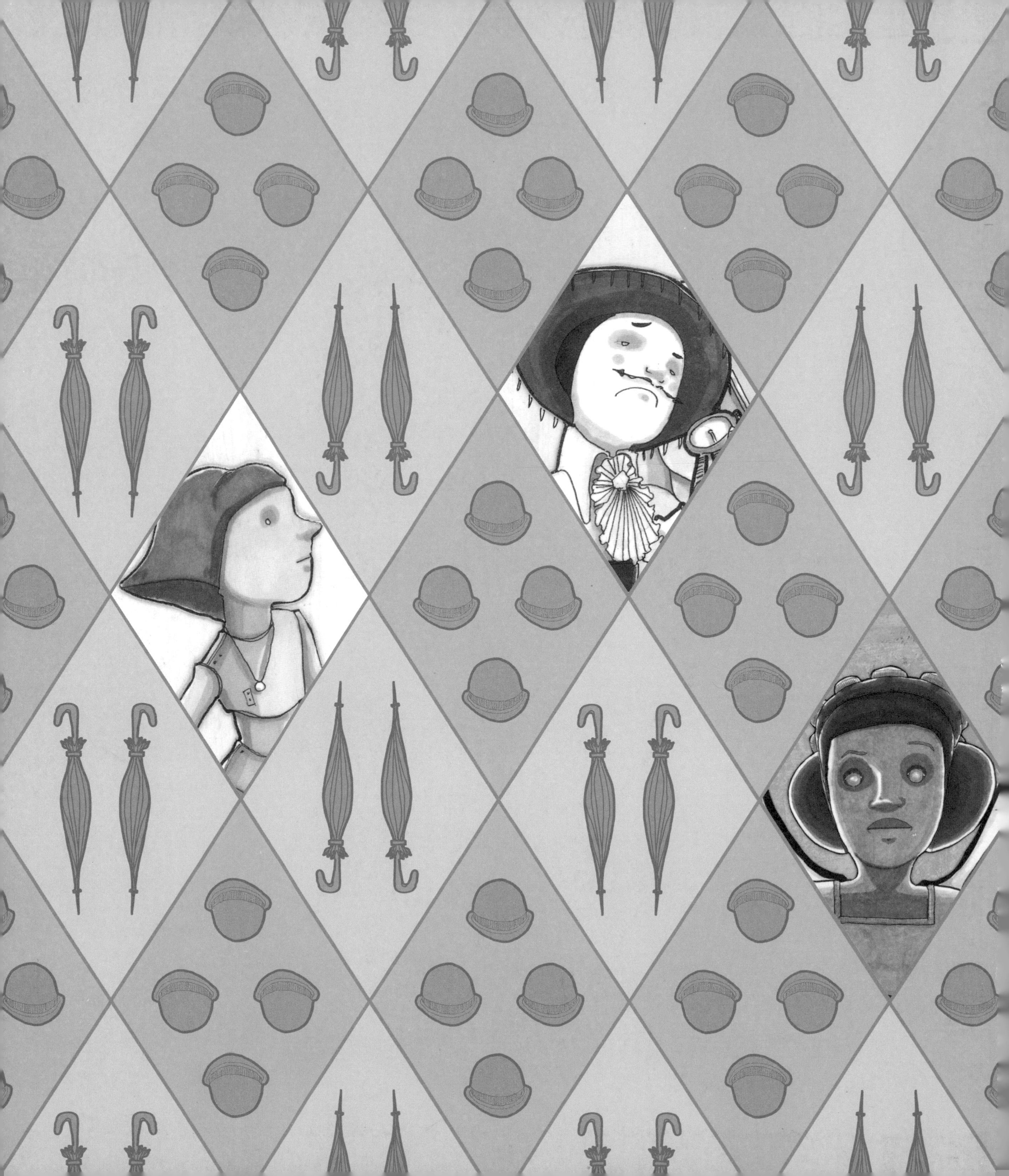